Friends

A Space Coast Writers' Guild Anthology

Edited by Scott Tilley

Friends

P.O. Box 262

Melbourne, FL 32902

www.SCWG.org

Published by the Anthology Alliance

**Anthology
Alliance**

An imprint of Precious Publishing, LLC

Precious Publishing
www.PreciousPublishing.biz

ISBN-13: 978-0-9979456-2-1
ISBN-13: 978-0-9979456-3-8 (ebook)

TABLE OF CONTENTS

DEDICATION

To Watson, my new best friend

PREFACE

An incomplete angel named Clarence once told a despondent banker named George, "No man is a failure who has friends." Whether your friends are people, diamonds, or dogs, friendship is the basis for a happy and successful life. According to the musical theme from the popular TV show, friends are there for you – always.

Throughout our lives, friends come and go. I'm fortunate to still be in contact with some of them from my childhood. That's me on the cover photo, taken in 1969, with my best friend Richard. I'm the one on the right with the awesome haircut.

This year I welcomed a new friend into my life: Watson. He's a rambunctious Golden Retriever puppy that is turning nine months old this week. In the five months since I've had him, my life has changed significantly – and for the better. For example, I'm forced to step away from the computer at regular intervals because he wants to play toss or have his belly rubbed. At first I found his interruptions annoying; now I look forward to them. He's a healthy reminder that there's a lot more to life than just work.

This anthology from the Space Coast Writers' Guild (SCWG) is a collection of stories about friendship in all its forms. The Guild is a network of writers dedicated to the same goal: helping authors realize their writing ambitions. Since 1982, the SCWG has provided activities to educate, develop, and promote its members. Visit www.scwg.org for more details.

Scott Tilley
Melbourne, FL
December 20, 2016

ACKNOWLEDGMENTS

The Space Coast Writers' Guild relies on the efforts of its many volunteers to bring projects like this book to fruition. I would like to thank members of the SCWG's Board of Directors for taking their time to plan and manage the anthology during our project meetings. They were also invaluable in providing their assistance during the review process. I am also thankful to outside reviewers for their comments on Board member submissions to the anthology.

A very special thanks to Donna Chesher for her help with editing the book. Through her expertise, the anthology was much improved. Any remaining errors in the text are purely my responsibility.

Lastly, thanks to all the writers who submitted their work to *Friends*. Without them, this wonderful compilation would not exist.

FRIENDLY ADVICE

By Christopher Robin Adams

"It's an island, babe.
If you didn't bring it here, you won't find it here."
Quinn (Harrison Ford), *Six Days Seven Nights*

Typically, when my wife and I take a Royal Caribbean cruise, I will take a few hours in this island or that to find quiet time for writing while she visits the beaches with friends or reads on the ship or catches rays by one of the pools. A liter of water from a dripping ice chest; an overflowing margarita from a bare foot islander; a writing bag with book, journal, pens, and cigar; and an open mind will cover me for Coco Cay. A White Russian and a few shots of espresso along with the latter two will feed my creative muse in most of the other islands and ports of call. I like to meet the local residents, which I can do in odd coffee shops, small restaurants, and local bars. I gain the perspective of a different culture, a different set of historical references, and an invigorating take from those who meet the public day after day, year after year. These, and the fun days at sea for dancing and dining, return us to cruise after cruise.

Ten or fifteen years ago, in the early years of our cruising, I met Brooks. He had a small booth on Coco Cay and custom carved onto shells scenes of the sea or tourists' names or any picture requested. He later expanded into bottle decorating and other craft areas. The shells, though, held my attention, because every other booth sold ready-made items from the islands or distant shores. When I collect souvenirs, I try to find the unique, memorable, and personal; this way, it will find a place in the home and assist me in recalling its source and the people or events surrounding it. Alastair Reid, translator of Pablo Neruda, (p9, *Absence and Presence*, 2009) described the found-things Neruda placed around his house as "…extensions of his own imagination, the vocabulary of his poems…." I, too, touch the found things on my shelves, walls; I, too, recall the past as I reframe it with new references. Gazing at Brooks as he worked

1

evoked the memories of past "acquisitions;" I use that word specifically, because the purchase is immaterial, but the bringing into my life and home of memories of friendly people and colorful cultures enriches and expands my life.

That day, I picked a small tiger cowry with a typical islander fishing boat with billowing lateen sails and three small figures aboard. From what I have seen in the Caribbean, they were fishermen preparing to set nets, though the dark sky suggested they had pulled them up and were heading in before a storm. The lateen was first used around 200 CE by Arab sailors, and its use spread throughout the Mediterranean and pushed ocean-going sailing as it permitted ships to sail into the wind. Many of the non-moneyed ships I have seen throughout the islands have been like this ship image. I chatted with Brooks as he worked on other shells, and I noted the attention he gave to each. Yes, I thought, this would be a good item to have back in Florida.

Heading toward the back area of Coco Cay, I wandered past palms and flowers, vines and grasses, birds and iguanas, as well as tourists and their families. Several areas exist with tables and counters upon which I can plunk my bag and set a drink or two; from that vantage point, I might look into palmettos and see birds dart through them, upon the beach to see wavelets lap its shore, or up to the horizon within which sail fisherman or other cruise ships. The air may be hot, but the drinks and palm shade do a fine job of making it tolerable and spurring good writing.

After a few hours, I head back to the ship, taking a short detour to bid farewell to Brooks, if he hasn't packed up his goods at the end of the day. If he is still there, I might share a poem or two, and I might give the backdrop of the poem and reflect in the telling how I see him receiving it. He regularly becomes my first audience: is my story getting through. I don't write highbrow; I write for the people walking the street beside me, dodging others on the sidewalk to get to their destinations. The tender takes me back to the ship, and my wife and I clean up for dinner and more dancing. I share writing and items from the shops and tell the accompanying stories.

Over the years, the patterns of movement onto and across the island have become a backdrop to the more interesting news I find in talking with Brooks. We might discuss a book, a story, a magazine article, or the news. He is happy to see me without being effusive. Five years may pass, eight; it doesn't matter. I have mailed him poems and see them stuck to the walls of his booth area. Friends I have sent to see him mention the poems.

With this as my back story, I arrived a couple of years ago on Coco Cay and sought Brooks out. We talked and as I prepared to head back toward my writing area, I turned and asked, "What should I write about today, Brooks?"

He looked at me with his kind eyes appreciative for the question, "Friends."

"OK," I replied, paused, turned, and walked away. How interesting, I reflected, and how insightful. From his very different background than mine, he has the same questions, the same interests as I have: what does it mean when people seek each other out after years, when they stay to talk with an acquaintance while family and friends wait, when unprepared topics are brought up just to find what another mind thinks and what another person feels?

For a near off-the-cuff comment (I think of the term as referring to casual and unserious), life seemed to take another dive beneath the surface of this sunny and blue skied island. The poem below came forth from the muse that day, and I shared it with Brooks as I passed by on the way to the ship.

***

Friends

Dedicated to Brooks,
my friend and inspiration in Coco Cay, Bahamas

Sea grapes park beside my driveway:
      chartreuse, green, and dark-green,

large-circle leaves shine skyward on fingered branches
　　　　that strike out from sturdy trunks
　　　　whose heights reach 20 feet and beyond,
　　　　but whose flexibility dances easily in hurricane winds;
their bunches of jam-quality, sweet-burgundy fruit hang within easy
reach.

These trees and their richness exist when I am home,
and their qualities grace earth as well
　　　　when I cross the Indian River Lagoon to the mainland.
They grip Florida's sandy soil without me,
and hold tight to our sand dunes without me,
and tower over railroad vines as they drip seeds without me.

Friends exist in our world
　　　　as people dancing and talking along earthy or esoteric lines,
　　　　cavorting and helping each other with the burdens of life,
　　　　　　　　or alone
　　　　walking a beach or holding a shell,
　　　　parking by dunes in sea grapes' shade or by pastel, slim-leaved
sea oats.

Like cells with potential, friends prepare themselves for action;
like Zen monks, each allows no blockage.
Open to receive,
　　　　built to share,
a friend welcomes his world in trust,
invigorates her universe to encourage.

Beside my driveway, sea grapes sway in light breezes.
They are what they are.
An example of Abraham,
they offer copious shade and provide delicious fruit,
build lumber-worthy trunks and rattle their leaves

when requested by the wind
or another force of our planet.

I can say the sea grape is my friend,
but it might question me:
      its candor completes its mission,
      my blockage impedes mine.
In a dance with the Tao Te Ching (34),
      we scarcely understand a touch of greatness,
      we barely and slightly grasp friendship;
if we partner with the sea grape,
      we become the sea grape
      and a friend.

***

I reread the poem now, thinking that we sacrifice for friends, but we do not do so in such a way that we become less of who we are. With friends, we give of our authentic selves. When asked, we give honest opinions; we do not volunteer unsolicited suggestions to change the other person into our image because they offend our sensibilities of the moment. Think of that person when you met him, when you first got to know her. Sometimes, we don't want to see others grow in new directions; friends do not have that impediment.

The poem and Brooks' suggestion for it periodically return to reorient my thinking. As I look forward to a cruise sometime in the next few months, I also look forward again to dancing and dining with my wife, to enjoying the sun's yellow billowing around me, to leaning my head back as the breezes cool me, and to chatting a brief bit with an old friend, a good friend, Brooks.

#

Christopher Robin "Kit" Adams released his first collection, *Spanish Cedar*, preserving the art of the cigar experience, in 2014. Professionally published in the Florida Educational Leadership Journal (2011), his poetry has appeared in numerous literary journals. He was a poetry judge for central Florida writing groups, a National Writing Project Mentor (1997), a first place winner in poetry for Space Coast Writers' Guild (1999), and a recipient of the Distinguished Service Award for SCWG (2000).

AN EXTRAORDINARY FRIEND

By Anne Bonner

All alone
I lean on you
my husband's joy

Together riding in Florida's
sunshine, planning
life's events

Such happiness, delight
and gladness
never knowing God's plan

You are all that's left
Wind blowing, dark clouds hovering
sad song in my heart

I step on the gas
fly through the afternoon storm
melancholy mist

Raindrops falling
mixing with my tears
my husband's pride

Lending an ear, offering musical tunes
My buddy and best friend
his red Mustang convertible

# # #

Anne Bonner, a fifth generation Floridian, has written nine historical fiction books in nine years. Turning from prize winning essays and poems, Anne wrote the Florida Pine Haven series, five Y/A books set during the Civil War era. She has now written four books in an adult series of love and intrigue set during the same era, with plans to complete the fifth book soon. Active in several writers groups, Anne also served on Space Coast Writers' Guild board.

BEST FRIENDS

By Shaun Bonner

I have a best friend
Who is truly my friend
In the thick and the thin
In the rain and the wind
She beams like the sun from ear to ear
Each time our company draws near
Though we are different, her short and me tall
We have the greatest friendship of all
Together we spend hours at a time
Without even speaking a line
We share friendship's truest essence
To simply enjoy each other's presence
So take care until next time I see ya
My beloved Eskimo dog, Reba

#

Shaun Bonner, grandson of Anne Bonner, is a Florida native. At fourteen, he reached the rank of Eagle in Boy Scouts. He graduated from Cocoa Beach Junior/Senior High and the International Baccalaureate Programme. He now attends the University of South Florida as an honor student majoring in industrial engineering. He's also an Army ROTC cadet, so upon graduation he will commission as a second lieutenant. He hopes to remain in Florida in the National Guard.

MOBUTO

By Glenn Boutilier

I want to go to Mobuto
But I don't know how
It's a place not found
On any map
Nor found
In any book

I have a friend
Who lives there
She's waiting
Waiting just for me

Not so very long ago
And very much alone
I sailed a wooden sloop
To a deserted tropic isle

As I walked along
The soft white sand
A giant red sun
Rose from the sea

Waves of foam
Chased sandpipers
Bleached shells
Shaped like angel wings
Lay beautiful in death

In the froth
Of the surf

A bottle rolled
Back and forth

A struggle
To escape
The firm grasp
Of the sea

Worn and pitted
It must have drifted
On an endless highway
On an endless tour

I saw within
A rolled up scroll
A message in a bottle

I pulled the cork
To gently extract
The precious artifact

Hello
My name is Mashika
It means rain
I live in a hut
Made of grass
In the village of Mobuto

A sickness came
To our village
And now I live
All alone
Won't you be my friend?

#

Glenn Boutilier is a Suffolk University of Boston alumnus, former school teacher, business owner, and ex-tour guide for the movie stars homes in Hollywood. Current projects include two novels soon to be published: *Troll Trouble* and *Zombie Fever*. A short story thriller called *Illuminati Hitman* was a semi-finalist for a Royal Palm Award. Membership includes: Florida Writer's Association, Space Coast Writer's Guild, Space Coast Fiction Writers, Cocoa Beach Writer's Workshop, and the Key West Poetry Guild.

FRIENDS AS A NOUN

By Maria Capella-Miller

Friends! It is a beautiful noun with positive feelings that bring to mind an echo of understanding, support, nurturing and love. Friends and love can't depart from each other. Who is my best friend, you may ask? As a teacher of languages, I will answer this question using a grammar structure: The very first pronoun in the conjugation of any verb is "I."

In Mark 12:31 we are reminded to "Love your neighbor as yourself." I understand the premise of this statement is that I have to love myself first, getting along with the person that I am. Being my best friend means that I treat my body and my intellect with TLC (Tender Loving Care). Intentionally, I practice a healthy living full of choices. What I eat and drink are good for my body. I nurture my mind with thoughts that are positive and encouraging. I also exercise. This cocktail of behaviors is nothing new as that's what the doctors have been recommending for centuries. I surround myself with people that lift me up, and avoid those that bring me down. I haven't known a person that can love others without loving himself/herself. Keeping a yes attitude in life can help a friendship to blossom. When I start from "the friend I love the most is I," my perspective about friends open wider for inclusion. This is not a self-centered idea, but one that creates the conditions for me to be a lifter and not a leaner.

Khalil Gibran in his famous book *The Prophet* wrote: "Friendship is always a sweet responsibility, never an opportunity." As I begin recruiting people to be part of my circle of friends, I become more aware of the responsibility of giving more than receiving, even though receiving automatically becomes part of the equation. This philosophy begins to work with everything in life because giving turns energy back to you!

For me, in the "University of Friends" lessons began early in life. There were multiple friendship classes, some of them seemed happy and some were definitively painful, some were worth repeating, some stayed as thorns to be taken out and forgotten. As I grew older more learning took place. I repeated some classes when the lessons were not easy to learn, but the outcomes were the same; then, I made a greater effort until I was able not to repeat prior mistakes, to pass to a better level, and to move on because to obtain a solid Friendship's Degree all the elements and structures have to be in place: compatibility, loyalty, good character, growth, and love. With this degree in hand, I just became more selective.

In my journey through the process, I learned that friends are not just people. When we define a noun, we recite this definition: People, places, and things. Let's go over each one of them:

People that I can count as friends, besides myself, two for sure whether we are close or apart: Ken, the person with whom I married many years ago, and Gustavo, my son. The miracle of birth transforms mothers into providers, nurses, teachers, counselors, and eventually it progresses into friends. I have dedicated my life to these two people in every shape and form. In return I get an amazing response of all the elements mentioned above, including love, loyalty and trust. With them, I have traveled a road of ups and downs, and have been able to handle and manage the curveballs that life throws, just because life is a big game full of loses, gains, and lessons. Their friendship is steady and firm.

Even though I am an extroverted person with a friendly and pleasant personality, it is not easy for me to expand my circle of true friends. It has to do with Post Traumatic Stress Disorders (PTSD) symptoms from friendships that have left a sour taste to say the least. Sentiments of deeper caution arise now when making friend choices. There is a saying in Spanish, "nos vemos las caras pero no los corazones," which translates "we can see each other's faces, but we can't see each other's hearts." We can't anticipate what the intentions of other people are. Betrayal and deception have happened to human beings for thousands of years. In fact, Jesus experienced them, coming from members of his own inner circle. Simon denied him three times in spite of the fact that he had been chosen by Jesus to build his church to continue his legacy. Simon acted out of fear, and perhaps we excused him, but what about Judas, one of his twelve disciple-followers who acted out of greed? These two examples illustrate how the intangible laws of friendship have been violated forever…and yet, we all give friendship another chance.

When a noun in a sentence structure has to do with places, friendships can be applied and built upon. I am a friend of this country, the United States of America. As such, I hate to hear episodes where people that are welcomed by the generosity of this huge and beautiful land, turn around and hover feelings of destruction and terror after they benefited from an education, and after being exposed to better working conditions, human rights and equal opportunities. For this friend of mine, I work hard to make a living and to give my tax contribution. I am never in trouble with the police and other authorities simply because I obey the laws, the written and unwritten ones. I don't join conversations to put this country down, I just have to remember how things are managed in the country where I came from, and that cures any negative thoughts. I always believe that in order for Americans to understand how good they have it here, they should live for at least two years in another country, developed or underdeveloped. Basic things such as not throwing trash on the streets are part of my behavior toward this place that I treasure with gratitude. I was born and raised in South America, expanded my education in the United States and had the fortune to see the beginning of a new generation carrying my blood. President Kennedy left us a famous quote that has resonated in my mind forever: "Ask not what your country can do for you; ask what you can do for your country." It is easier to think that a friend is a person, but it takes vision to sculpt the idea of having places and things as our friends.

When I was around ten years old and for a few more years, if I behaved wrong in the eyes of my parents, they punished me by sending me to a room that they locked in the outside so I couldn't get out. Meals were brought to me during three days or a week, according to their judgment of the offense. It is called child abuse in the United Sates; back then my only thought was that I deserved it.

There was a wall in that room covered with books, and that was the good part of it because out of idleness I read and read to no end. Charles Dickens and his Tale of Two Cities took me to incredible places and situations. Grace Metalious and her book Peyton Place introduced me to intrigues and dramas full of passion and twists. I traveled into deep waters with Herman Melville with his novel Moby-Dick. Books became my friends for good. They were there without judgments to keep me company. They entertained me and held my hand to pull me out of feelings of abandonment and depression. I didn't care about their age. Old or new, I just loved my book friends. The relationship between them and I have continued for decades, as they have been there for me, just waiting for when I am ready for their company, and I have been there for them to grab and embrace them as the minutes become hours. They have allowed me to live the dramas that they bring, with the reassurance that I don't have to carry the dramas with me when they go back to the shelves.

My book-friends have helped me grow personally and professionally. I have read some of them more than ten times, such as when The Greatest Salesman in The World written by Og Mandino came to my hands. I memorized its scrolls, and they became my mentors in life. Since then, I have "welcomed each day with love in my heart." Stephen Covey taught me how to get organized in his masterpiece The Seven Habits of Highly Effective People. Once this book became my friend, I began approaching time wisely, trying to stay on "Quadrant Two." My listening skills improved, and my understanding of other people to add value to them became greater. Wayne Dyer taught me to move from the past to the present, and not to blame others for the outcome of my own choices. That happened when he brought to my attention Your Erroneous Zones. I read each one of his books and learned because there are no better mentors than these friends. The list of authors that have contributed to my formation can go on and on. These are the kind of friends that are welcomed to enter into my world of silence to speak loudly through their black print with the hope that I visit them from the beginning to the end.

People, place, and things! Now you know about my friends. I am excited to know about yours.

###

Maria Capella-Miller is from Cartagena, Colombia. She published the fiction novel *Exilio Voluntario* (Self-Imposed Exile) and the compilation of short stories *Los Secretos de Mis Amigos* (my friends' Secrets) where she gives personification to birds, turtles, and dogs. She is a college language teacher and a John Maxwell speaker and coach, where she helps others to get to the next level. Contact her online at www.4us2grow2gether.com.

THAT BOY

By Iris Culhane

He was a boy. He was my cousin and he was wild. He became my best friend.

I was in the living room listening as my mother and grandmother talked about *that boy*. *That boy* was my cousin Clark. He and our recently widowed Uncle Bill would be moving into our grandparents' New York City apartment in a few weeks.

"I don't know if it's such a good idea, Mama, taking *that boy* in. Bill will be gone all week at his out-of-town job and he'll be no help. From what I hear from his Aunt Helen out in Pennsylvania, where they've been living, Clark is a pretty bad boy," my mother said.

"No such thing as a bad boy—only folks who don't understand him," Grandma replied.

"Well, that may be but the stories aren't good. He played hooky, stole milk money from a kid at school, chased the chickens out of their pen, and who knows what else."

I could hear Grandma's soft chuckle. "Let's just wait and see. He's only eight. He lost his mama just a few months ago. Maybe all he needs is some love and understanding. He'll get that here, turn him around."

When the shrill whistle of the teakettle drowned out their voices and I couldn't hear much more, I left the sofa, hoping to join my thirteen-year-old sister Gloria and her best friend, Lorraine. They were sitting on the floor of the living room whispering and giggling as they moved the pointer across the Ouija board.

When I got closer Gloria stopped moving the pointer and hovered over the board. "What do you want? This is private," she said.

I backed up and stammered. "I won't bother you. Just wanted to see what you're doing."

"Well, you saw and it's really something you wouldn't understand. Why don't you go in the kitchen and help your grandma with the snacks," Lorraine added.

Head down, I retreated to the sofa. It was always this way. Gloria and Lorraine were an inseparable pair. They never included me. I was too young, only seven, they were always talking about boys and clothes and their favorite movie stars. Grandma, my mom and all the aunts and uncles admired Gloria. She was pretty, kept her clothes neat and got good marks in school. Everyone was proud of her.

I was different. I liked to go to the park, feed the squirrels, climb trees—do the kinds of things that got my clothes and me dirty. My marks in school were just average. Guess nobody was proud of me. I felt like I didn't belong.

I longed for a close friend, someone like me, someone to do things with. I knew I had a cousin about my age but I don't remember seeing him. His mother was sick and she didn't like to travel or see too many people. My grandparents visited Clark, his mother and my Uncle Bill sometimes but they never took me with them. When I first heard he might be moving close I was excited. Maybe we could be friends. After hearing what my mother and grandmother said I gave up on that idea. Now I was even a little scared to see him. We definitely couldn't be friends. But I knew I would have to meet him.

I came to my grandparents' house the day Clark arrived. "Is he here," I whispered when my grandmother opened the door.

Grandma pointed to the living room. "In there, putting things in his room."

I tiptoed in and quietly sat on the sofa watching Clark bring his belongings into the small bedroom. He was tall, with blond hair standing up in greasy spikes, and a dirty scowling face. He moved cartons from the living room to the bedroom, dropping them on the floor with loud bangs. I tucked my legs under me, scared but fascinated by his anger and energy. When all the boxes were finally placed Clark took two giant strides, reached the sofa and kneeled in front of me. I shrank back against the cushions trying to make myself small.

Without a word, he leaned forward, smiled, stuck out his tongue and wiggled his ears. Forgetting to be scared, I gasped, "How do you do that?"

Ignoring my question, he rose and pulled me up from the sofa. "C'mon," he said as he grabbed my hand and guided me to the door. When our grandmother asked where we were going, Clark said we'd be back soon and without waiting for a reply began racing up the stairs. I followed. We started on the first floor and continued to climb. The sound of our footsteps echoed off the steps of the marble staircase, and on the third landing a dog barked. Clark was fast and I couldn't keep up. At the fourth landing he stopped. "Almost there, one more to go." He reached for my hand and slowed, allowing me to set the pace.

When we reached the door to the roof he paused. "Ever been out here before?"

I had, but always with an adult. I simply nodded. He opened the door and the creaking sound was so loud I jumped afraid we'd be caught. As Clark quietly eased the door closed, I cringed. What was I doing up here, alone with this bad boy? Maybe he'd pick me up and toss me off the top. I turned my back to him, about to wrestle the heavy door open and flee.

He took my hand and urged me forward. I resisted. "Hey, don't be scared. Nobody will know. Let's look down, see how small everything is from up here."

Not knowing why, I followed him as he dropped my hand. I took a few steps forward then froze as he moved to the edge, bent over, and looked down. He turned back and gestured. "It's nice. Think I'll walk around." He now had one leg up on the edge of the roof. Terrified, I ran toward him, grabbing his arm and trying to pull him back.

He laughed and quickly got down. "Scared you, huh? But I made you come closer. How do you like the view?"

Fascinated and losing my fear, I whispered, "It's great."

Clark took a penny out of his pocket and held it over the edge. "Let's see how long it takes for this penny to reach the ground."

I watched as the coin plummeted down, landing on the curb.

Clark took another penny out of his pocket and handed it to me. "You try it."

I hesitated. "What if it hits somebody on the head? It would hurt."

Clark poked me in the ribs, "Look before you throw, now go!"

We threw pennies. Then Clark started to spit over the edge. "C'mon, watch, it'll never get to the ground."

I watched and he was right. The spit took off in the breeze— never going very far. I joined him and it was great. We were careful and jumped back when we saw someone looking up. Tired of testing the laws of gravity, we sat on an old crate someone had left behind, and talked.

Clark was serious now and asked, "Grandma and Grandpa seem okay but will they make me do chores? Will they knock me around if I'm bad?"

I gulped wondering if he'd been hit a lot, before I answered. "You'll probably have to do a few things like take out the garbage or help carry packages. They're pretty easy-going, though—especially Grandma, and she never hits anybody. She just has this way about her that makes you want to please her. You'll see. She's a great cook, too, and when you do something good she smiles and give you an extra cookie."

Clark looked happier now. "Oh, that sounds better than living with my aunt Helen in Pennsylvania. She throws a mean punch."

Hearing that made me sad. "You won't get punched here. And

you know what else? One of the best zoos in the world, The Bronx Zoo, is really close. We can walk there. Maybe we'll go soon."

"That would be great. Living here might not be so bad."

By now I had lost my fear and I asked, "Did you really do all those bad things they say you did?"

"Probably, but I was mad a lot, I hated everybody. Maybe it will be better here."

"Hope so," I said.

We were quiet, until Clark asked who my friends were. I lowered my eyes, "Have none."

Clark laughed and I looked up at him. "Neither do I." Then he wiggled his ears.

"Can you teach me to do that—wiggle my ears?"

"Probably not. They say it's some weird inherited thing. But I'll try."

After working with me for about five minutes he gave up and shook his head. "Didn't work. But we can try again some other time."

We spent a few more minutes talking then realized we should return to Grandma's apartment. We went back as friends.

When we opened the door we were faced with my red faced, scowling mother. "Clark, where did you take her? We looked all over the neighborhood, even the park. Where were you?"

Deciding to take the blame, I lied. "Sorry we scared you but Clark didn't take *me* anywhere. I took *him.*to the schoolyard. Showed him where to line up, and then we went to the candy store for a soda. Were we gone long?"

"Yeah, you were. You absolutely were. Don't ever go off like that again without telling me. Now go ahead. Wash up, Grandma has some milk and cookies for you both, although you don't deserve them."

On the way to the bathroom, I punched Clark on the arm and stuck out my tongue. He laughed. "Liar. But thanks."

Clark and I lived only a block apart and we spent lots of time together. He was generally the leader in risky adventures but I usually found a way to explain our dangerous activities. Clark admired my skill and called me a "house angel and a street devil."

We did so many crazy things but never got caught and hardly ever got hurt. I do remember one really close call. The super hero Superman was very popular, and since Superman's alter ego was Clark Kent, my cousin Clark decided to use his name and shock some of our friends. He was a speedy runner and one day, facing a glass door of an unoccupied store, he backed up about twenty feet, stretched out his arms and shouted, "Faster than a speeding bullet" as he raced toward the closed door. We had rehearsed this and he intended to stop just before he reached the door. It was a bad plan. The momentum carried him forward and he crashed though the glass, leaving an imprint of his arms and body. Shards of glass were everywhere. Blood trickled from the many cuts on his body. The kids who had gathered to watch were shocked into silence.

I helped my cousin home and got him into the bathroom before Grandma could notice, then began picking splinters of glass out of his face, arms and body. I grabbed a towel and dabbed away at the cuts—none were deep. We tiptoed out and stayed away until all the bleeding stopped. By the time we returned only a few wounds were visible. Clark told Grandma he'd fallen and I told the same story. She never knew the truth.

Sometimes my cousin helped me. I wasn't a great student and hated to study. When I failed a math test, and had to have it signed by my parents, Clark hunted around and found a paper with my mother's signature on it. He brought it to his room, spent a few hours practicing, and then copied the signature. No one questioned it. After that, Clark helped me with math and my work improved. I didn't need to have any more tests signed. The forgery remained our secret.

Everything wasn't always wonderful with us. We had our share of childhood fights too.

When Clark went with my dad on an all-day fishing trip to Montauk, New York, and left me behind, I was jealous. I hated my cousin. When I went with them on their next fishing trip, all was forgiven.

Another time Clark was jealous of me when his dad gave me a gray striped kitten after my old cat died. He quickly got over it because the kitten liked Clark better than me and we shared its care.

The four years we spent together were a very memorable time that ended when my uncle remarried and moved to another state with his new wife and Clark. By this time we had matured and had many of our own friends.

Our special friendship gave us confidence and made us stronger in so many ways.

I joined the chorus at school and became the lead second soprano. My grades improved, and I convinced my mother to let me chose my own clothes—not the frilly ones I hated. I made the summer swim team, and won several races. Most importantly, I lost my fear of my bossy sister, and stopped trying to follow her around. We got along better, even cooperating by putting our funds together to buy our parents an anniversary present.

Clark lost most of his anger, and restless energy. He stopped defying simple rules and muttering curses under his breath. He even helped Grandma in the kitchen when she was baking cookies. He constructed intricate balsa wood model airplanes, which he proudly hung from the ceiling on nylon strings. His natural leadership qualities and charm made him one of the most popular guys in the neighborhood.

Our special bond remains and we still keep in touch, especially on our birthdays. Clark and I are eleven months and three weeks apart, making us the same age for one week every year. It's another unique thing we share.

I never learned to wiggle my ears.

#

Iris Culhane has always believed in the power of storytelling—it could be in the form of a poem, a short story, or a book. She has been writing these stories all of her life. Now retired from teaching up north, she has more time for her passion and has recently completed her first novel. She lives in Florida with her husband and their devoted Australian Shepherd, Redford.

ON FRIENDS AND FRIENDSHIP

By Yolande Donnelly

The Greek Philosopher Aristotle wrote that there are three kinds of friends:

1. Friends of Pleasure (includes friends with whom we enjoy various kinds of activities together, such as sports, games, etc.).

2. Friends of Use (friendships that develop based on mutual needs, such as colleagues at work).

3. Friends of Goodness (friendships based on soul connections).

My definition of friendship includes a fourth kind of friend:

4. My life partner (the one person with whom you share the most during your life).

Friend of Pleasure

When I was young, I remember my first important friend, Diane. We went to school together, lived next door to each other, and were best buddies. We did everything together. Diane had many older sisters, and as they taught her how to dance, cook, and other things concerning growing up, she passed her new knowledge on to me.

I was invited to join her family in her summer cottage in rural Quebec, where we spent many weekends together. Diane saved my life from drowning and she also introduced me to my first husband Andre. Her auntie gave both of us our first real jobs together. We were close in every way.

After I got married, I moved away and our friendship faded. We were both starting families and we never got together again.

I remember her fondly, but I realized that when I disconnect from people as a rule I move on and form new friendships. I live in the moment and share each passing day with people and activities that I have in front of me.

My favorite quote describing this is "Love who you are, love where you are, and who you are with."

Friends of Use

During my years of studying, I made several friends who were going through this activity with me. My choice of friends was based on mutual need rather than attraction. For example, Margaret-Marie and I studied Italian together for several years. We had little in common other than this activity, but it was intense enough to form the basis for a friendship based on use. Efforts to expand our friendship to include leisure activities like traveling together and family gatherings were less successful, and it was obvious that our friendship was essentially one-dimensional. When our studies were over, the friendship dissipated.

Friends of Goodness

I have a lifelong focus on spirituality, and in my search for that I have developed many long-term relationships with several friends. While I could include them in the category of friends of use, I differentiate this small group as having more substance and tenure than the normal study friends. For example, my friend John and I have traveled together, attended conferences and spiritual gatherings together, and conducted a long-term dialogue on our spiritual paths together. John is a good soul, and our friendship is concentrated on that area of our lives. The rest of our lives are really not discussed.

My Life Partner

To some degree, all friendships are based on attraction, and in the case of my life partner, Jim, we are both number one to each other. I have witnessed so many fractured partnerships, and unsuccessful partners, that having this friendship is my most satisfying and wondrous experience in my life.

Jim and I fit together. We share everything, both trivial and important. Our most important life experiences have generally been together and our shared memories over forty-plus years have formed that glue that will keep us together for life.

In my view, each of us has a limited capacity for sharing our lives, and in my case my life partner willingly takes up the lion's share of my friendship quota. His is the friendship where my needs and his are kept on an equal footing, and the give and take necessary for living together in friendship is carried on gladly by both parties.

* * *

For the most part, I keep my own counsel, so I do not seek a friend to fill a need for providing or sharing advice on how to conduct my life. I invite friends into my life to share activities and knowledge and to celebrate living together. However, I believe that if we want to have good friends, we must first of all be our own best friend, like the motto "Love yourself, and other will love you."

Past experiences have taught me to measure friendships as an investment on both our parts, and when I take up a new friend I go through a process of determining how I feel about that person, their needs and capacities, and my own ability to make a commitment to the friendship.

Ending friendships hurt, but I have experienced that nothing lasts forever, and friends fade away as the cost of maintaining the friendship exceeds the pleasure of carrying it on. Leaving a friendship may be growing in different directions, establishing different beliefs, changing mates or other life altering circumstances. In my case, changing countries from Canada to the US caused several friendships to fade away. Friendships generally require geography to flourish.

Can we be "just friends" with the opposite sex? In my view, the answer is a limited "Yes", but the opportunity for sexuality is often lurking just around the corner, waiting for the most inopportune time to pounce, which can place a great stress factor on the friendship. Only friendships based on a soul connection that brings you closer to God can weather the more mundane qualities like sexuality.

As we grow older, our capacity for friendships gets smaller. Our reduced energy level takes its toll on everything in life, including maintaining friendships. We must let go of some relationships that become time and energy robbers. Finally, friendship deal-breakers include breaking trust with friends, moving to break other's relationships or just plain loss of interest.

"Friendship is like a bank account. You cannot continue to draw on it without making deposits."

#

Yolande Donnelly was born in Montreal, Canada under the sign Libra. She is retired and is now a permanent resident of Central Florida with her husband, Jim. She speaks four languages and has a Master's Degree in Esoteric Science. She has taken up creative writing as a hobby, concentrating on fictional short stories. Her latest work is *12 Lives, 12 Signs*, available at Amazon.com. She can be contacted at yolandedonnelly@icloud.com.

AN ESSAY ON FRIENDS

By Kevin Doyle

Friend (Eng) . . . also Ami (Fre), Amigo (Spn), Freund (Ger), "Droog" (Rus), Sadiq (Ara), Pengyou (Chn), Dost (Ind)

Examining a Social & Psychological Phenomenon

What can I say?

Like money. I've had some, lost some, and wish I had more…they come, they go, I have a little power over them, or they have a lot over me. It never lines up just right.

My initial foray with friends starts like anyone else's…in the early days, it's not much more complicated than, "oh you like to breathe? So do I, let's be friends!" And there it is…a couple six-year-olds with the world at their feet. In time, it's baseball cards, ridin' bikes, shooting hoops in the backyard, hanging out after dark, vows to always hate girls, Little League, chillin' on Friday nights, camp, movies at the mall, and summer weekend getaways with other moms and dads (be on your best behavior!) Those idyllic adolescent years just roll on by. Pending dad's big job changes (the inevitable cross-town, -state, -region, -country move), events track along somewhat predictably.

Soon hormones, high school, and the opposite sex appear…the pot stirs. Uncertainty or the great maelstrom, frequently in the same hour. Friends are there…a bit like Travolta's pals in Grease. Sometimes goofy, awkward and unpredictable but you have your go-to network. And, always a "Sandy" to mess with your head. Friday night football games, the mixer afterwards…"great band, do ya think she'll dance with me?" Double dates…when they go to the bathroom, you're comparing notes…"you really like her?" Keep blinking…a prom or two, then graduation…sign the yearbook, "have a great summer, how did we make it through Algebra, we'll always be friends…don't forget me!" But you do. And they do. Wilted petals from a flower.

33

Then college…the second big friends reboot. New people, new influences, the old you morphs into something else. At Christmas break my freshman year, I called a few of my high school pals up and said, "I have new college friends now. They're more my style! I wish you the best. I won't be coming back after this." True story. Figured (most inaccurately) I'd never see them again. But, oh the new friends, even other dorm buddies…a few older ones too. I mattered. The older sibling(s) I never had! They came by to look for me on Saturday nights! Never would have predicted that.

Blink some more…senior year, graduation closing fast. Mom and Dad wondering what I'm doing with my life…I have no idea. Some of these great college friends have now faded from the scene…either quit higher learning or (the older ones), graduated. One or two married…her? Really! Say what? What happened to those great weekend nights, the parties, hanging out in the girls' dorm after hours…the girls we got drunk over…the girls we…you know(!). Comparing hangovers on Sunday mornings. Great times, now gone. Whoever heard of four years being measured in a few passing seasons? Me, just me. I didn't want to leave.

But you have to. Careers now…gotta justify paying for that major. Even if it was the wrong one! I'm in the Midwest, they are way out west. They might as well be in the Sea of Tranquility. We write letters, but in time, lose track. Grad school or crummy first post-college job…more opposite-sex drama. Now my old friends have gone and made little humans…no time for me. I have to buckle down. Earn money. I have work associates now…but friends? Not sure. Some after work drinks…watch them females scarf down that wine! Things might get interesting. And a couple times, things do! But, three months later, I walk out the main entrance with cardboard box and some personal effects. I never hear from them again. The job sucked anyway. I'll always remember Lisa and that band in the lounge.

(Rinse and repeat some variations of the above paragraph about seven or eight times over thirty years. So, I got plaques on the wall, some signed pictures "great having you on the project or good luck wherever your future pursuits take you." Like the yearbook scrawls and promises, they too are ghosts in the mist.)

In mid-twenty-something angst, I call a few of those high school pals I blew off those years back. I'm a curiosity now ("well, look who's back...home from the far West.") "You ditched us twice, first when you went two thousand miles away to school and then remember that weird Christmas phone call?" "Yeah, yeah...what can I say?" How about, "I'm sorry." A couple of parties to try and catch up; awkward from the get-go. I drink too much or not enough. They have new friends who give me the "who the hell are you" look. But, it's not the same. The thing about parallel universes, they don't intersect.

The future spouse appears...just like the country western song says, "when I wasn't looking or I was down and out or when I was at my worst, but there you were." (Pick your musical context.) She/he sees a kernel of hope in you. You hope they are right. Whether they are either your carbon copy or fill in all the missing spaces, it seems to work. Your own little human beings start to appear. You find your happy little family are all good friends now. Both the better half and the miniature extensions of yourself. Laughter, toys under the tree, vacays, Little League, soccer, first bikes, first phones, first loves, report cards, SATs...I found out my daughter was quite the budding musician. Introduced her to all my 70's and 80's music...she could do pretty good renditions with guitar and piano. I had ideas...a future Bonnie Raitt or Sarah Bareilles? Time would tell.

Then the boys came and her brain turned to oatmeal for a while. She survived, found equilibrium but a job, her own wanderlust, her own "trying to figure it all out" reared its head. She left home in her early 20s and that was that. We're still friends, and I miss her dead-on "Seems Like Teen Spirit" power guitar. She took her gear, Nirvana posters and (appropriately) moved to Seattle.

My son, also a best friend for a while...we used to watch Mystery Science 3000 Theater and laugh at the robots and the bad movies. Although somewhat an introvert, he has a helluva dry sense of

35

humor. His tersely worded, droll 'tm's' split me up. He got a first job at Wendy's because the manager was impressed with his Clash T-shirt and knowledge of the band. Then Joe Strummer dies about six months later. How messed up is that? Then college, about three majors before he settled on a final one…trips to New York City with his pals…you and I know I'm losing a second one. He's only a thousand miles away now.

Brothers and sisters…well, there was a gaggle of us for sure. Being the oldest and with some of the travails I've been on, I have no clue how they look at me anymore. I was friendly with them at various times, but with them all younger and other interests, talents and influences, you could find yourself the lost sheep fairly easily. Not a black one, but a lost one. Five of them and one of me. It's OK, they are all decent enough people and I wish them and their families the best. Mostly I get a Christmas card. We didn't have to be 'besties', we just had to survive adolescence.

Then there was Dad. In the early days, he was what I wanted to be, although I had no idea how to get there. Always witty, strict, demanding, had a way with words, a gentleman, a faraway look in his eyes…he understood the machinations of the world. Then in high school and college, I found him obnoxious, my nemesis and in my face non-stop. How can I be in trouble so damn much? I think I'm still grounded for stuff I did back then. I started to re-appreciate him when I was on the north side of fifty. But there was a clock ticking in him – and not in a good way. While I couldn't equal his success, I did find my own groove, which toward the end he gave me decent props. As you're always trying to please the old man, I was honored.

He survived the triple bypass, but the diabetes in the background was eating him up. And his doctors being American doctors, they prescribed lots of Ambien and Oxy-something or other for the ten other issues that were chipping away at him. He'd fall asleep in mid-conversation because he was wide awake at 3 a.m., by himself. Then the phone call…"we lost dad earlier today." I had talked to him on the phone about five days previous. That's 120 hours. He seemed OK. Weak but OK. But no more conversations now…. he 'got' me,

36

and I think I finally 'got' him. I had to do his eulogy which I wrote one that was a decent send-off, but I came close to losing it at the podium. My delivery did the words no justice. I miss him as I type this.

Then there's Mom! Her gift to me, was translating angry Dad, frustrated Dad, "at wit's end" Dad, psycho Dad in those dark days. At the time I thought I had a lot of reason to write him off, that we'd never be on the same page, but she was; "no, he's just trying to make you better." And after a time, she was right. On top of that, other than a minor peccadillo or two, she was always patient with goodness and loyalty to her kids and an always upbeat outlook. When it's time for her to shuffle off this mortal coil and join Dad, that will be another eulogy I will dread giving.

But you say to me, "well, it's not all bad…the Internet, Twitter, Facebook, Facetime, suckface, face-off, save face, etc. are all there to stay in touch with your friends and associates, right?" You just sign up for an account, list your interests (drinking and watching YouTube music videos) and all the great places you've gone or want to go. So what…I go places, you go places. My vacay pictures are as bland and uninspiring as yours. I can make a witty commentary on things I think about or see on TV ("that Miley Cyrus has some talent but she is crazy.") Oh wait, I'm supposed to list my influencers too. Nobody influences me at this age! I don't even know what those are. Then virtual and infrequent real friends occasionally check-in and add some of their pictures of other humans and places I don't know and comment on my comments. So I got no one to have a drink with, but I have a gaggle of people commenting on my pithy Miley Cyrus comment. Whatever. Yeah, 21st century friendship…just like James Taylor/Carole King sang about in 1973, right?

But there's one other one, right? Yes, and that would be the Mrs. Her thirty-five years with me…the "Waring Blender." The sometime Village Idiot. The occasional sane man in the insane world. The selfish, easily angered, chip-on-his-shoulder, "I'm right and you can all go to hell," underachieving, little person I can be. Her kids are gone, and I'm no prize these days. I know they were her best friends.

And I can't fill that void. I try…but there are insufficiently precise words to say, "I'm sorry they are gone, but I can't turn time around to bring them back." All we can say to a loyal spouse who will still fix our lunch after three and a half decades is, at best, "we're sorry and thanks for taking the ride with us." And it's those days that I'm alone in the Sea of Storms.

So—this treatise has gone a curious route. My only insight is this: maybe the best friendships are the most difficult ones. And when you bleed, scream, cry, agonize, question, botch their eulogies and mourn time's distance, I think those are the ones who will help get you through the relentless madness of life.

It's been that way so far.

# # #

Kevin Doyle is 'quasi-retired' from the defense and private sectors and resides in West Melbourne, FL. He has self-published a novel, *Galen's Kids* (a retrospective about college) and a short-story in the Space Coast Writers' Guild 2016 anthology, *Spring*. He graduated with a bachelor's degree in English from Indiana University. He and his spouse, Elizabeth have two adult children living in Indianapolis and Seattle.

AMAZING GRACE

By Cindy Foley

Monday, 8:17 a.m. Phyllis was late for work. It didn't matter a whole lot, seeing as how her husband Rick was the boss. She wasn't in any big hurry to get there either. Monday mornings weren't their favorite times. He'd left the house, grouchy as usual. A weekend never seemed to be enough time to get things done that needed doing; mow the yard, grocery shop, clean the house, change the oil, wash the cars. Self-employed, they had seven employees and projects up the ying-yang; she ought to be more grateful for that. She'd tried telling him how fortunate they were to have these kinds of problems. All he could talk about were the problems he'd have to solve today. Everyone's mistakes fell on his shoulders. Didn't she understand that?

Oh yeah, she understood that alright. He'd told her enough times. When would she ever learn to just shut-up, but no, she'd told him right back about how she didn't need to hear his crabby remarks early on a Monday morning, and right after she'd fixed him a nice breakfast and packed his lunch too. Every day was filled with stress and worry. Where had the fun and the laughter gone?

The day had barely started and already it was cranking up to be a doozy. The twenty-five-minute ride to work gave Phyllis just enough time to bend her older brother's ear, listen to some sage advice, calm down some. She put the Bluetooth in her ear and told Siri to call.

The phone connected on the first ring. "Hey, what's up?"

"Got prayers?"

"Again?"

"Yup."

"It's Monday, you ought to know better by now."

Phyllis sighed. "I know. The weekend went by so fast. I can't seem to catch a break."

"He probably feels the same way."

"Yeah, you're right." Something suddenly registered in her brain. Back a-ways, she'd seen something out of the corner of her eye. "What was that?"

"What was what?" her friend asked.

"I don't know. I think I saw a dog in the ditch."

"So?"

"I think it was laying in the grass at the top of the ditch, right close to the road."

"And?"

"What kind of a stupid dog lays next to the road? I have to turn around."

"Uh oh."

"Talk to you later." Phyllis threw her cell phone on the seat, swung to the right as far as was safe, and then did a one eighty, and floored the pedal. About half a mile back toward home, there it was, on the left now, a little black little head peering out of the grass as cars zoomed by. It didn't move. Strange that.

"I bet it's been hit." At the next space between the speeding cars, Phyllis veered across the road, pulled into a driveway, jammed the car in park, and ran in high heels to the dog.

As she approached, it tried to stand but fell over onto its side. "Aww." She kneeled down beside it. Blood; whining; a too-big collar with a name engraved on a silver tag, Gizmo, the fuzzy pooch raised its head and looked at her with the most beautiful deep-brown eyes she'd ever seen. Phyllis immediately fell in love.

They'd never had a dog, had talked about it once or twice, never seemed to make it happen, though. They were too busy.

Another lady dropped onto the grass beside her. "Aww. It's been hit. I can help. I always carry boxes in my car just for this sort of thing."

Phyllis suddenly felt possessive toward the dog. "That would be great," she answered. "And, we'll put her in my car. I pass an emergency veterinary clinic on my way to work. I'll take her there."

"Okay, I'll be right back."

Within minutes, a crowd had gathered. A wide, concrete sidewalk ran for miles along the other side of the ditch. It was a popular road for dog walkers and joggers. Everyone had ideas. "Anyone have a cell phone? Try calling the number on the collar. See if you can locate the owners."

Phyllis gently petted and soothed the dog. "Gizmo? Is that your name, huh? You're going to be all right, Gizmo."

When the helpful lady returned, she ripped the box and lay the cardboard flat on the ground next to the injured dog.

"It looks like her back end is the worst," Phyllis said.

"I'll pick her up by the front," the lady said. "On the count of three, see if you can lift her back end just enough to get her onto the cardboard, and then we'll carry her on it to your car."

"Good idea."

It worked. Within minutes, they had maneuvered the dog and the cardboard stretcher onto the back seat.

"Thanks," Phyllis said and got in the front behind the wheel. Morning argument forgotten, she called Rick. The kind of guy who saved turtles on the road, and lizards trapped in the house, and spiders too, she knew if he'd found a hurt dog in the ditch, he'd have done the same.

"Let me know how you make out," he said.

* * *

It took Phyllis ten minutes to get to the emergency clinic. During the drive, she alternated between singing "Amazing Grace" and "B-I-N-G-O, and Gizmo was its name-o." She couldn't see the dog on the seat; prayed it was okay, didn't think about what if it weren't.

She pulled in at the clinic, got out, and opened the door to the back seat. The brown eyes briefly opened and then closed again. Still alive. She smoothed the fur along its side. "I'll be right back. Don't be afraid. You're going to be okay." She gently closed the car door and sprinted across the parking lot.

A woman behind a high, semi-circular counter looked up when Phyllis entered. "Can I help you?"

"I have a dog in my car. It's been hit. Can you help me bring her in?"

"I'll get one of the techs to come out."

Two veterinary technicians followed Phyllis to her car. When she opened the back door, Gizmo opened her eyes, raised her head, and whined.

One tech bent down. "Oh, she's cute. She's a young one. Not much more than a puppy, I'll bet." She ran a hand over Gizmo's side, gently picked up the rear leg. Blood streamed out of several holes and lacerations. Fur was missing around the ankle and up to the knee on the other leg. Whine. "Aww, she's a girl." The tech looked up at Phyllis. "Is she yours?"

"No, I was on my way to work and saw her in the ditch. I stopped and a nice lady helped me put her in my car. I pass your office every day on my way to work, so I brought her here."

"We can't take her."

"What? Why not?"

"Are you going to take responsibility for her care?"

"Can't you bring her inside and let's see how bad she's hurt?"

"Not without someone agreeing to pay."

"What kind of #*$! is that?"

The vet tech stood. "I understand how you feel, but you have to see our point."

"And that is?"

"If we didn't get paid for every hurt animal someone brought us, we'd go broke."

"Unbelievable. This *is* an emergency clinic, isn't it?"

"I'm sorry."

"What should I do?"

"Take her to the pound." The two women walked away.

Phyllis knelt by the open back door of her car and petted Gizmo again. After a few minutes, she picked up her phone off the front seat and called Rick. He'd know what to do. He always knew what to do.

"I'll call you right back," he said.

Five minutes later her phone rang at the same time as the same two ladies were coming across the parking lot. "I called Animal Control. They called the clinic and told them to stabilize the dog."

"Thanks honey, they're coming out to get her right now."

"All we're going to do is sedate her, clean her up, and bandage her," one tech said. "Someone from the animal shelter will come and get her later."

Phyllis hated leaving, but half an hour later there was nothing more she could do, so she went to work. All day long, pretty brown eyes stared at her from the corners of her mind. She called the phone number on Gizmo's tag several more times but got no answer.

"Stop worrying," Rick said. "They'll take care of her."

But, what did that mean? Would they take x-rays, see if anything was broken, fix her up? Or, were they going to euthanize her? Rather than suffer in the ditch, at least she'd have a humane death. Phyllis slammed her pen down on the desk top. What had she been thinking when she'd put the dog in her car? She had no idea. She'd just reacted. All day, she immersed herself in work, phone calls with clients, employee questions, looked at the clock a hundred times, thought about the dog, thought about the dog. Stop thinking about

43

the dog.

By the time she got out of work, it was after six. The Animal Control was in the opposite direction from home and probably closed anyway. No, she'd done her part. Animal Control was taking care of things now.

She and Rick were too busy to have a healthy dog, let alone an injured one. They'd probably put the injured dog to sleep anyway. Forget about it.

"I'm sorry for being so grouchy this morning," he said to her over supper.

"It's okay. I hate Mondays too."

"Friends?"

"Friends." Phyllis stared at her plate. "What do you think happened to the dog?"

"I don't know."

She thought about it all night, tossed and turned in her sleep. In the morning, the little dark eyes woke her up. At work she envisioned them again. Even the employees were asking if she knew anything. "That's it," she said. "I'm going to call them."

* * *

"She just came out of surgery," said the receptionist who answered the phone.

"She did?" A fleeting thought crossed her mind. Did I think she'd be dead? She dug her fingernails into her thigh.

"Yup. We've got a young married couple, both veterinarians. They volunteer on Tuesday mornings. They looked her over, took some x-rays, and decided they could fix her up. Only things is, she needs a foster home while she convalesces. Can you do it?"

"Oh my gosh, I don't know, um, I have to talk to my husband. Let me call you back."

"We can't keep her here."

"Can she walk? Can she go to the bathroom by herself?"

"Yes."

"Oh my gosh. I'll have to call you back. What does foster mean?"

"It means that she needs someone to take care of her for until we see if she heals well enough for someone to be able to adopt her."

Light at the end of the tunnel. It didn't have to be forever. If the dog didn't heal…what? She would give her back? What if she healed? Phyllis would give her away? Sure. She could do that. She headed to her husband's office and told him.

"How will you manage?"

"Fostering the dog sounds logical," Phyllis answered. "It's only temporary. We could bring her to work, make a place for her behind my desk. The lady at the shelter said she was going to have to stay calm for a few weeks anyway. They'll give us sedatives for her."

"How long would it be for?"

"Six to nine weeks at the most."

"And, then what?"

Phyllis sighed. The man always asked so many questions. His attention to detail was probably what made him so successful in business, but personally…? "I don't know. I'm going to visit her today."

Later that afternoon, when Phyllis arrived at the shelter, the veterinary assistant escorted her to the back where Gizmo lay recuperating on a blanket. The big brown eyes looked up as soon as Phyllis entered the room.

"Awww," Phyllis dropped to the floor beside the bandaged dog. "She looks great!"

"Yes, she came through the surgery quite well. We had to do what's called salvage surgery. We removed some bones and knitted the muscles on her back side to the upper thigh muscles in the hopes that they will grow together to form the support she needs for that leg. Actually, we're more concerned with the ligaments on her right side. Ligaments don't heal. We repaired the torn skin, and as you can see, we've put a cast on it. We're hoping that a ball of calcium will grow around the joint and support the ankle in place of the ligaments."

"Wow, that sounds complicated."

"She can walk," Dr. Paul, the veterinarian, lifted Gizmo and set her on all four legs. Still woozy from the anesthesia, the dog stood, wobbled a bit, but did not fall over. "She's already been out this morning. I figure she's about six months old, a definite advantage to the healing process. Youth is a wonderful thing, especially in this case."

"Amazing," Phyllis said.

"Let's go up front and finish the paperwork and get you out of here as quick as we can."

Phyllis shook her head and opened her mouth to protest but stopped herself when glassy brown eyes looked up at her. The choice had already been made. "Oh, Gizmo…."

"Yeah, about that. Did you ever get a call back from the phone number on the collar?"

"No."

"Well, we don't think that's her name. The collar was really for a bigger dog. It could easily have slipped over her head without us having to unbuckle it. She just doesn't look like a *Gizmo* to us. We were hoping you'd rename her. Any ideas?"

Phyllis stuttered. "How about, Angel?" She fumbled about in her brain for a good name. "Or, Gracie? That's it, Gracie."

"Gracie, it is."

The whole thing was escalating out of Phyllis's control. It had probably never been in her control in the first place. Amazing Grace, how sweet the sound....

Twenty minutes later, they'd packed food, meds, and the convalescing dog into the back seat of her car. She headed to Molly Mutt's Thrift Store for the benefit of the Humane Society and purchased a large crate, a water and food bowl, and a quilt.

* * *

When Phyllis got home, Rick helped get Gracie out of the car. "She's pretty," he said. That's what everyone said when they saw her. The puppy settled in behind Phyllis's desk very nicely, and calmly remained there for the first week, except for the coming and going home and the occasional assisted hobbling to go outside to do her business.

By the end of the second week, a sparkle had returned to her eyes and a shine to her coat. A minor annoyance, Gracie developed a habit of barking whenever clients came into the office. Once she let everyone know a stranger had infiltrated her world, she'd again settle down to her diligent efforts of watching the backs of her eyelids.

Mornings and evenings, Phyllis and Rick tiptoed around the house and whispered in soft tones. Softness developed on their stress-pinched faces and gentle smiles came more easily. Gracie wasn't the only one healing.

After a month, she discovered the once-a-day sedative was in the peanut butter and spit it out. Wrapping it in a piece of bologna didn't work either. Rick joked. "Maybe I should start taking it."

Once a week, Phyllis drove Gracie to the vet where they checked the stitches and changed the cast. By the end of the fifth week, Gracie was working on chewing it off. She was rapidly developing into a bright eyed, lively, puppy with a vibrancy that belied the fact that a car had mangled her entire back-end.

During the sixth week, Dr. Paul took the cast off, and Phyllis took Gracie for her first walk. It was only around the half-acre yard, but the venture was a success. As her strength returned, Gracie walked around the office, visited the employees at their desks, or sat by the full-glass door and quivered at the site of squirrels playing in the grass on the other side of the parking lot. Phyllis continued giving her daily therapy and stretching exercises. By the end of the ninth week, although still limping, Gracie could walk half a block and seemed to love every minute of it.

"Time to adopt," said the lady at the shelter. "Let us know soon if you're going to keep her or not. And don't feel the least bit guilty if you decide to give her up. She's a sweet girl. I'm sure we won't have any trouble finding her a home."

Phyllis's heart thudded painfully in her chest. Give her up? This was the moment she'd been dreading. How could she give up the sweetest thing that had happened in her life since chocolate ice cream? No, she had to think logically. Gracie was becoming more active by the day. Even though every employee had fallen in love with her too and took her out for walks when Phyllis couldn't, the frisky puppy still barked every time clients came in. And, her favorite chew toys were Phyllis's shoes.

"We travel a lot," Phyllis said.

"We can give you a list of dog sitters."

"We own a business."

"How have you been handling it these last nine weeks?"

Phyllis had to face two more hurdles; her own doubts about whether or not she wanted the responsibility of a dog, twelve to fifteen years of vet bills, shedding fur. She realized the list was rather short. And then, what about Rick? He'd have all the same objections she had, and more.

But, he didn't. "You might as well keep her," he said. "She's probably better company for you than I am."

Phyllis was stunned. She couldn't remember having seen her husband smile so much. If not for this happy, energetic mutt, Monday mornings would still be miserable. The house would still be as neat as a pin, but Phyllis wouldn't have a walking companion. Rick was leaving the decision up to her. She knew what that meant. She'd be the one scooping poop out of the yard, running Gracie to the vet, training her to come, to stay, to fetch. It'd be like having a kid in the house again.

Gracie nudged Phyllis's hand. "Keep me," those brown eyes begged as if she knew what Phyllis was thinking. As if there'd ever been any other decision to make.

The next day, she took Gracie to the shelter to say her last good-byes and to complete the paperwork. Just as Phyllis was about to sign, her cell phone rang.

"Hello?"

"Hi, I'm calling about a sign I saw on the road about a found black dog."

What?!

"A couple of months ago, me and my family went to Orlando to visit friends, and when we got back our dog was gone. We live near where I saw that sign. I'm wondering if it's our dog."

Phyllis's husband Rick had posted that sign the first week after finding Gracie. She'd forgotten about it.

"Describe her to me." The description matched perfectly, right down to the collar.

"That wasn't hers," he said. "That used to belong to another dog we had."

This couldn't be happening.

"We can't let you adopt her if they are the owners." The shelter manager reached for the phone. "Let me talk to him."

Numb, Phyllis listened to the one-sided exchange.

"If she's yours, you'll have to pay for her medical expenses."

Silence.

"Five thousand dollars."

More silence.

"You've got twenty-four hours to pay the bill or relinquish ownership."

There was no way Phyllis could pay five thousand dollars for Gracie's care. No one had told her about that part.

"Okay, she's going home with her foster parent tonight. You want to speak with her again?" The manager handed Phyllis the phone.

"Where do you live?" Phyllis asked. The address he gave her was two streets over, right in her own neighborhood. "Can I stop and see you on my way home?"

"Sure," he answered.

A half hour later, when Phyllis pulled into the driveway, a man and woman, and three little girls, each one approximately six inches taller than the next, all blonde and curly-haired, came running out of the house.

Phyllis's heart dropped into her stomach. There was no way she was going to be able to disappoint them. She got out of the car and introduced herself. "Want to see her?"

"Yes." The little girls crowded around the car.

"Be very careful. She was hurt pretty badly." Phyllis opened the back door.

"Aww, Lily." The girls climbed into the back seat, cooed over her, and cuddled her, and all the while Gracie's tail thump, thumped against the seat.

Phyllis looked up at the man. "Lily?"

"That's her name. We have her sister, Daisy, too. They were litter mates. Lily has always been an escape artist. When we came home, we found that she'd chewed through the rope."

"So, what are you going to do?" Phyllis asked.

"There's no way we can pay the expenses. We just moved here and spent all our available cash on rent."

"Does that mean you're going to relinquish ownership?"

"Do you want her?"

"I was just about to sign adoption papers when you called."

The man looked at his wife, leaned over and glanced into the back seat, and then nodded.

"I'll go down tomorrow and sign the papers to give her up. Come on girls."

They were very obedient and climbed out of the car. "Good bye Lily." One bent over and kissed her.

"Stay," Phyllis said when the smallest girl got out last. Gracie…Lily stayed.

* * *

And that is the story of how one dog changed so many people's lives. The only fee the shelter charged Phyllis was the spaying and adoption fee of $50. Three months later, she and Rick paid $5,000 for a chain link fence that Lily promptly learned how to climb over. They spent another $100 to thread an electric wire through the chain link and buckled a shock collar on Lily's neck whenever they had to leave her home.

That was six years ago. Lily has since learned that staying in the yard is better than getting shocked while trying to climb out, that Rick is the one with all the treats, and that Phyllis is the go-to gal for meals and walks. Lizards and squirrels are for chasing. Couches are meant for afternoon naps and shoes are off limits.

Lily brought warmth where once there'd been stress, and smiles where there'd been frowns. But most of all, Lily brought friendship to Phyllis and Rick, and turned their house into a home.

"...I once was lost, but now I'm found, was blind, but now I see."

#

Cindy Foley is the author of *The Truth Lies...a Florida Saga*, a historical fiction based on a true story. She is also co-author and photographer of *Chase A Dream Today*, the poetry chap book *Water Drops*, and the published short story *From Heaven or Homeless*. She is currently working on another novel, *Snow on Evergreens*, a historical fantasy, and will publish a novella *I, Clawed: The Renewal of Bling* for Christmas 2016. Cindy is Treasurer of the Space Coast Writers' Guild and editor of the Guild's monthly bulletin. Her short stories and poetry have been published in the SCWG anthologies, *Gratitude*, published in the fall of 2015, and *Spring*, published in the spring of 2016. She is also an organizing member of the Brevard Authors Society. You can contact her at cindyfoley123@gmail.com.

BEST FRIENDS

By Terri Friedlander

When Jenny first set eyes on Kirk, it was love at first sight. Never before had she seen anything so amazing, so perfect, so loveable. Everything about his sweet face made her want to reach out and trace her fingers over his soft skin, button chin and adorable cheeks. And those golden strands that graced his head reminded her of her own mother's wispy hair. Captivated beyond words, Jenny had never seen another living thing more delightful than Kirk.

Until that moment, she had led a charmed life and didn't want for anything. With a bedroom fit for royalty, closet loaded with clothes, and surrounded by family who adored her, Jenny had little to cry about. Accustomed to the spotlight, she loved the constant flash of cameras and video taken of her every move. Her existence resembled one of those storybook fairy tales she dreamt about.

But suddenly her eyes were fixated on this remarkable creature. She'd never be alone again. Deep down she knew, Kirk was destined to be her best friend.

As though in perfect agreement with her thoughts, when she dared to put her hand on his, Kirk grabbed it as though he'd hold on forever.

And then he let out a toothless squeal of delight.

And then he let out a toothless squeal of delight.

At six days old, Kirk became Jenny's own living and breathing doll. She wanted to pick him up and rock him in her skinny arms like one of her Cabbage Patch Kids. She overheard their mother say the two were "Irish Twins". Baby Kirk was the greatest birthday gift a precocious one-year-old girl could ever ask for. Her life would be changed forever.

Kirk came into the world looking like a cherub with a smile painted on his face. Little did she know then, her brother was born without a fear factor. And without a mean bone in his body.

In no time, they were holding hands and running to play together at parks on the slides and swings. Celebrating birthdays and holidays by each other's sides, the two fresh faces were a photographer's dream, worthy of an Ivory soap commercial. With her wavy blonde curls, frilly pastel dresses and polished Mary Jane shoes, five-year-old Jenny posed as though rehearsing for the runway at a young age. She loved playing dress up and owned dozens of Disney princess high heels to match.

When he turned four, mischievous Kirk sported a rough-and-tumble hairstyle that barely saw a comb. Always laughing like the happiest child on the planet, he loved racing his Big Wheels and climbing trees, making holes in his new clothes seconds after getting dressed.

Yet, whenever her brother would fall and scrape his knee, Jenny appeared close behind to pull him up and brush him off. Just call me, little bro, and I'll be there, she whispered one day, wiping his tears.

She cherished Kirk's bear hugs, how his face lit up when he looked at her as he tried to repeat her big words. She'd give him piggyback rides and read him stories. Jenny delighted in going to the local amusement park together, building sandcastles at the beach or just having fun with their toys at home.

Even when she bossed him around playing 'school' with her as the teacher, of course, he'd smile, sit at his small desk, raise his hand

and laugh. Kirk's endearing disposition earned him the nickname, "Sunny Fella".

Throughout elementary school, she kept her eye on him, acting as watchful and protective as a second mother.

For years, Kirk seemed to idolize his big sister as though she too were his best friend.

Then, without warning, around her twelfth birthday, when heading off to middle school, sibling rivalry reared its ugly head. Suddenly, Jenny began finding everything about her brother infuriating. She'd complain that Kirk got more attention, a larger slice of pizza or a taller scoop of ice cream. In reply, he'd share more with her and beg her to play or read to him.

Those awkward years plagued Jenny with a heap of insecurities. She hated her long legs, thinking she resembled a string bean. Her mood swings blew like the wind as her acne condition worsened. At the same time, she watched as Kirk seemed to get better looking and more popular.

Feeling like she didn't have one athletic bone in her body, Jenny observed with green-eyed envy as her brother mastered every sport in and out of school. Baseball, basketball, skating, skiing. Kirk seemed to love them all. On vacation one winter, he announced he was bored with skiing and wanted to try snowboarding. Frustrated and discouraged, Jenny struggled on skis down the beginner slopes. Laughing at her many face plants, Kirk led the way on a snowboard like a pro, the undisputed golden boy and Olympic star in training.

At fourteen, trouble lurked as Jenny's hormones raged with the tenacity of a riptide. Overnight, she became boy crazy, obsessing over the cool guys in school, wearing makeup and dressing in skin tight outfits in an effort to look older than a ninth grader.

"Were you flirting with that jock, Brad, at recess today?" her friend Diamond asked when they were in her bedroom after school one day.

"Quiet, big mouth. That's the one I was telling you about. He's a great kisser. He told me that I'm beautiful. He even called me his girl."

"No way, Jenny. Isn't he like three years older? Are your parents going to let you date him? I can't date till I'm sixteen."

"Me either. But my parents are too busy following Sunny Fella's baseball schedule to even notice."

"If I didn't know better, I'd say you were jealous of your little brother."

"You have no idea how Kirk can be so annoying. My parents act like he walks on water. He's the favorite all right."

"But he's really nice. I wouldn't mind if Kirk asked me out. Didn't he just turn thirteen?"

"Huh? You just said you can't date. And that would be too weird. Forget it."

Just then, Kirk opened the door and walked into her room, a big smile plastered on his handsome face. He held a bowl of potato chips in one hand and a bottle of soda in the other.

"Ever hear of knocking," Jenny told him.

"Hey, Diamond. Want some chips? What are you two gossiping about?" Kirk ignored his sister as he sat on the floor to join them.

"None of your business. You can't just barge in my room."

"We're talking about Brad Green. Do you know him?" Diamond reached for a handful of chips.

"Sure do. From softball camp last summer. He's bad news. The coach had strict rules about no drinking or drugs. Every day, Brad bragged about getting drunk before games. And I'm pretty sure he showed up stoned a few times too. He's not good for you, Diamond. Stay away from that stuck-up guy. He thinks he's a gift to the world."

"Hold on, Kirk. I'm not the one interested in Brad," Diamond said coyly, tossing her head in Jenny's direction.

Kirk turned his gaze to his sister. "You like him, Jen?"

"Maybe. But don't tell mom and dad. If you do, then I'll tell them you took Dad's motorcycle out for spin when they weren't home."

"Sounds like blackmail to me."

"Whatever! You don't know everything about him." Jenny said without a smile. "And I saw you steal a few of dad's Budweisers from the fridge, too."

"What? Do you have eyes in back of your head now? When did you see me touch dad's "private stock"? Got anything else you want to hold over my head?"

"I know you sneak his scotch. I'll date Brad Green if I want to. Now get out of my room and leave the chips. And don't forget to knock next time."

* * *

At school the next day, Jenny searched the cafeteria for Brad. How dare her goody-two-shoes brother pass judgment on him?

Just as she had hoped, she found Brad at "their" table, surrounded by his buddies. Jenny greeted him with a kiss and sat by his side, feeling like a little puppy dog, trying not to drool. The guy was gorgeous. Perfection. Her know-it-all brother was dead wrong about everything. Brad wasn't a stoner or a drinker. She was left panting for his attention. It didn't matter what anybody said about a freshman going with a senior. This had to be love.

After lunch, she almost stopped breathing when Brad insisted on walking to her class and holding hands in the hallways. Ignoring the teacher while everyone else took notes, Jenny doodled and daydreamed about him the rest of the day.

At the last bell, he escorted her home, then kissed her neck and told her how much she turned him on. To Jenny, Brad's kisses were nothing short of heaven on earth.

She nearly fainted when Brad whispered that he wanted to teach her things, to be her first lover. Quivering at the thought, she didn't think life could get any better.

That week, she dodged Kirk's questions and his watchful eye. When Brad invited her to a house party on Friday night, Jenny couldn't believe her luck. Her brother had an away game that same night and the family would be home late.

After school on Friday, Jenny combed through her closet, discarding one outfit after another. She applied some of her mother's makeup and lipstick and finally settled on a pair of Guess jeans and a pink Abercrombie shirt that she thought made her look cool and sophisticated. Earlier, she had succeeded in convincing Diamond to sneak out and join her.

When Brad arrived, he brushed her cheek lightly after giving an approving nod, then introduced a friend who sat behind the steering wheel of an old jeep. If her parents ever found out that she had gotten into some stranger's car, she knew she'd be grounded for life.

By the time the foursome arrived at the house, a crowd had already gathered. Kids offered Brad high-fives as he strolled into the room like a rock star with Jenny on his arm. Music was blasting and kids were talking and laughing above the noise. Brad led them to a table with bottles of vodka, rum, soda and a keg of beer. He poured four red Solo cups full of rum and coke and made a toast. Jenny felt like she was on top of the world.

Brad's buddy with the car keys seemed enthralled with Diamond and Jenny watched as they disappeared into the crowd. Then some kid began passing around a joint and Brad eagerly took a hit. Surprised, Jenny stared at him without a word but he didn't seem to notice. This clearly wasn't his first time getting stoned. She had never tried pot herself and wasn't about to start now. One vice at a time, Jenny laughed, holding her first cup of alcohol.

Three cups of rum and a migraine later, the smoky room began spinning like a record on a turntable as Jenny's stomach began churning. Was this supposed to be fun? Brad had long since vanished.

Alone and nauseous, she needed to get home but didn't even know where she was or who to call. When she noticed it was after midnight, she panicked and left the crowded room to search for Diamond.

After locating her friend drunk outside in the backyard with a group of strangers, Jenny returned to use the bathroom and find a phone. Nothing could have prepared her for the sight of Brad sitting on the sofa, a blonde girl laughing at his jokes, leaning in to kiss him just as she walked into the room.

Her heart crushed to pieces, tears welled up in her eyes as she began stumbling around. How could Brad do this? They were a couple. The racket of kids waving their Solo cups in the air, screaming along with The Rolling Stones song *Can't Get No Satisfaction*, was making her head pound.

She ran outside again, bent over and began to vomit. All at once, she couldn't stop crying as she spilled her guts all over the yard.

At first, Jenny thought she was dreaming when she heard Kirk's voice calling her name. Out of nowhere, he handed her a bottle of Sprite and then swooped her up and carried her to a car parked in the busy street full of kids watching in amusement. In her drunken stupor, she held onto Kirk's neck, never wanting to let him go. When he plopped her down in the passenger seat, she turned to find Diamond, eyes closed, rocking back and forth in the back seat, looking equally pale and dazed.

Jenny never learned how her brother found her or cared to ask.

Kirk saved her life that night.

He had been right all along about Brad. About everything.

She guessed that's what best friends were for. And Jenny would never take hers for granted again.

#

Terri Friedlander was born and raised on Long Island, NY. She has dabbled with a notable list of job titles, including teacher, college professor, columnist, and MIS Director of the world's largest law firm where she traveled the globe. Terri is the author of *Work Hard Play Hard, Chasing Her Destiny, Torments and Triumphs of a High School Teacher* and the soon to be released novel, *The Dorm*. Loving life in Florida, she can be reached at www.terrifriedlander.com.

FRIENDSHIP

By Barbara Hanson

"Hold a true friend with both your hands."

– Nigerian Proverb

light in darkness
empathy in sorrow
acceptance in failure
joy in success
quiet in chaos
tight bond
that respects space

sharing secrets
uttering truths
hearing confessions
reading thoughts
with
 no words spoken

a different kind
of love
precious
to hold
tightly with hands
and
cherish with the heart.

# # #

Barbara Castle Hanson, M.A., M.S., co-authored the nonfiction book *Vermont: Wilderness to Statehood, 1748-1791,* and has written over 4,500 newspaper columns. She had poetry included in the summer 2016 issue of the national magazine *The Pen Woman,* and also in the Brevard Scribblers' anthology, *Driftwood.* Barbara is a member of Space Coast Writers' Guild, Scribblers of Brevard, Blueprints Critique Group, Florida Writers Association, the National League of American Pen Women, and the Poetry Society of Vermont. She loves writing, reading, and travel.

What Is a Friend?

By Jay Heavner

What is a friend? The word friend can be defined many ways. People we know on Facebook are called friends. Facebook allows up to five thousand friends per page. Some people have that many, most of which they don't really know much if anything about. I don't think that's really a good description.

So what is a friend? They come in many shapes and sizes, colors, and may not even speak the same language as you. The Bible gives us many examples of a friend. A Jewish man was beaten, robbed, and left for dead on the road to Jericho. Two men, also Jews, passed him by, but a Samaritan man whom the Jews hated, was willing to put himself at risk of attack from the highwaymen and rescued the half-dead man. It's easy to tell which of the three passersby was a friend. The Good Book also tells us, "Greater love has no man, than he will lay down his life for his friends."

We were traveling abroad. We stopped in a town and my wife tried to use a vending machine in front of a small shop, but it took her money and gave her nothing. She pointed this out to the shop owner who just shrugged her shoulders. A young woman, a local, saw what was going on, and said she would help. She proceeded to loudly barrage the store owner before the customers in ear shot. The missing money was quickly returned and my wife thanked the helper. She was a friend. We never saw her again, but her help will be part of our memory for as long as we live.

In war, a man will often lay down his life for his band of brothers.

Most people want their spouse to be their best friend. Some achieve this. Some don't. There would be much less divorce if the two could be true friends.

Some friends you may meet only once in your lifetime when they perform some act for you and ask nothing in return. Others may last for life and be willing to charge hell with you armed with nothing more than a water pistol. Some you may not see for years, but when you do, you can pick up right where you left off. That's a friend.

A fellow, on a job I once worked, gave me a definition of friend I never would have thought of. He wrecked a motorcycle and was in a body cast from the waist up. His arms were also immobile in an elevated position in the one-piece body cast. This did not stop him from going beer drinking with his buddies at the bar. He said, "You know who your friends are when they help you get rid of the beer you only rented." I would have to agree.

What is a friend? A person who's seen you at your worst and still stands with you. It's one that still knows and remembers you when you have a need and it will cost him somehow, small or large, to help you. Some say friendship is a mutual admiration that lasts. Whatever it is and however it's defined, I hope you have friends.

# # #

Jay Heavner is an award-winning author currently working on his fourth book, a Florida murder mystery to be called *Death at Windover*. His first three books, *Braddock's Gold*, *Hunter's Moon*, and *Fool's Wisdom*, comprise *Braddock's Gold*, a series about an Appalachian legend of a large gold payroll missing for two hundred fifty years, turning up in bits and pieces in 1995 and causing all kinds of havoc.

WOMAN'S BEST FRIEND

By Peggy Insula

Valerie couldn't cry any more. Her eyes stung; and although the grief remained, no tears did. She blew her nose, threw the Kleenex in the pile on the end table, and slumped in her chair. A television commercial about dog food caught her eye. Maybe what she needed was a dog. Her husband's death hadn't become any easier to bear over the last six months. The more she thought about it, the more she wanted a new best friend.

A few days later, when Valerie visited a friend's home, a jet-black, short-haired, Black-Mouthed Cur puppy, no bigger than Valerie's hand, convinced her to take him home. Darth Vader was friendly, playful, and easy to housebreak.

Living alone, Valerie justified bringing Vader home in part by her belief that he would grow to be a fierce guard dog. But when he grew to be seventy pounds of mouth and muscle, people shuddered at the sight of him—until he charged up to them and welcomed them with a sloppy dog kiss.

From the start, Vader was a lover boy, happy to sing and howl along at every opportunity and to greet every newcomer with an astounding solo vocal performance. He appeared to be proud of his range—he yodeled, smiled, and kept time with his tail. Vader's greatest delight was human presence—any human presence. So much for the guard dog.

Sadly, Valerie couldn't take him to work with her, so she came home every night to shredded pillows, ripped curtains, beheaded dog toys, and chewed-up left shoes (his personal preference—why? Who knows?). So Vader received a new doghouse for his six-month birthday and stayed in the back yard staring at squirrels while Valerie worked.

With Vader chained up to his new doggie condominium several hours a day, the backyard neighbor, affectionately referred to as Mrs. Bitchass Busybody, found a new interest to supplement her steady beer drinking. She sat on her patio in a quasi state of inebriation, as she did each day She couldn't bear to see the poor, sweet animal banished from the house so cruelly. After all, where *was* Valerie's humanity? At last, she heaved herself up, muttered, and stumbled into her house to make a call.

When Valerie arrived home that afternoon, an Animal Control truck awaited her in the driveway. A burly officer got out and opened Valerie's car door. "Good afternoon, ma'am. We got a call from a concerned neighbor about your dog. I'm here to check on him."

Valerie was extremely concerned—what had happened to poor little Vader?

After an hour-long tour of the backyard, the animal protector was satisfied that all was in order. Bidding the officer farewell, Valerie plopped down on her sofa to consider her next move. She'd show that meddlesome old crow across the back fence. In four shakes of a dog's tail, Valerie had a six-foot privacy fence installed and allowed Vader the run of the back yard while she worked.

A few days after this new arrangement, Valerie's friend Julie visited. Knocking on the door, Julia yelled, "Valerie, are you home?"

"I'm out back," Valerie called. Julie walked through the recently installed privacy gate into the back yard where she found Valerie leaning on a shovel and panting, a green bandana tied around her head. Julie looked down at the half-filled hole under the fence. "How many times has Vader escaped?"

"Four damn times in as many days. He needs a buddy. He's lonesome at home all day by himself."

Vader sat nearby, watching the hole filling with great interest and a sparkle of "I'll show you" in his eyes.

Julia plopped down in a lawn chair and eyed the puppy's innocent expression. "Are you sure about that? You could be asking for double the trouble."

"Oh, no. Dogs always do better when there's more than one of them." Valerie finished filling the hole and tamped down the dirt.

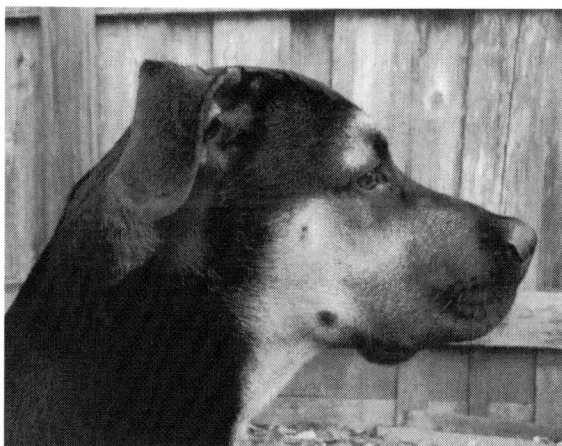

When Valerie came to accept that Vader, Casanova that he was, would never be the man-eating watchdog she hoped for, Valerie set out to find a companion for him. The next dog to capture Valerie's misguided heart was another Black-Mouth Cur at the local SPCA. Princess Leia was a little older than Vader and had raised a litter of pups at the shelter. Workers cried when Valerie took the sweet-tempered, caramel-colored dog home.

"You're sure to be a good influence on Vader," Valerie told her.

"He's still full of puppy foolishness, and you've already had experience teaching pups their manners."

Leia thumped her tail and smiled a smile that reached her warm golden eyes.

Vader raced around Leia in circles and barked with joy and excitement. Leia accepted his attention as her due and maintained her composure. Valerie exhaled. Everything was going to work out. Leia was going to keep Vader out of trouble. Thank God.

Sadly, instead of distracting Vader from more home-destruction, Leia enthusiastically joined in the fun. She especially relished helping Vader dig out under the fence. With two of them digging, they escaped twice as fast.

Three days later, Julia found Valerie unloading a truckload of cinderblocks in her back yard. Four large holes under the fence had been blocked with flowerpots and yard tools.

Valerie set the last cinderblock on the ground and looked up to greet her friend. "I'll be damned if I'll let these hellhounds outsmart me. After all, I'm the one with the PhD."

Julie chuckled. "Seems to me Vader is the one with a PhD—in Excavation Engineering. What are you going to do with all those blocks?"

Valerie adjusted her bandana tighter around her forehead to soak up maximum sweat and then planted her feet wide.

Julie, Vader, and Leia smiled and watched.

Valerie regarded Vader, the goofy, drooling culprit lying nearby, who apparently approved of the holes his owner was digging. "You're right about that. Vader could dig straight through to China or Bengali faster than I can finish this trench I'm going to dig all the way around the fence. I'm going to plant cinder blocks, two deep. Let's see if these damn &*@! hounds can get out then." She picked up her shovel and dug like John Henry.

Julie watched for a while and then wandered away.

Princess Leia was sweet and loving, but with hair bristled, she charged strangers in a way that left no doubt that their painful death was imminent. Leia was one fearsome warrior. Once, when the water meter reader came in the yard, she set her sights on the intruder's throat and came at him like eighty pounds of whip-ass.

Running out of the yard and leaning in panic against the gate didn't help Leia's victim because Leia bolted and jumped the six-foot fence like it was a wee hurdle in a racecourse. Only Leia's no-nonsense discretion allowed the retreating trespasser to live to see another day.

To Valerie's chagrin, Leia taught her special fence-vaulting talent to Vader, who was delighted to follow her lead in all things dog. Leia took a long, running jump up the corner of the privacy fence, used the middle support beam as a springboard, and sailed over it. Vader was a one-trial learner. Both dogs escaped nearly every time they were let out into the yard—every chance they got.

Valerie built another doghouse; now, both dogs were chained outside while she worked.

Mrs. Busybody, who, unfortunately, could see over the tall fence from her elevated patio, made another ranting call. Animal Control paid another visit, inspected, and gave their blessing to Valerie's doggy domiciles and animal maintenance plan.

On Julie's next visit to Valerie, she found her friend busily stapling two strands of barbed wire, at six- and twelve-inch intervals, above the top of the privacy fence.

"Let's see those cunning canine bastards jump the fence now." Valerie gritted her teeth.

After a couple of scratches and scrapes, Leia and Vader seemed to be dissuaded from jumping the fence. Valerie wore a smirk of victory.

Not long after, on a visit to a nearby farm. Valerie happened to meet Jaina, yet another Black-Mouth Cur: a young, skinny, yellow female. A one-year-old pup with topaz eyes, Jaina was a Velcro dog, attached to Valerie's side everywhere she went from the first instant they met. Valerie decided that since the containment challenges were going so much better with her other two dogs, she would adopt Jaina as well. On the way home, Jaina sat tall in Valerie's truck. And then there were three.

Jaina was a great listener—the best of the bunch. She hung on every human word and did her best to comply, but, it didn't take Jaina long to reveal her own God-given canine talent. She taught the other hounds how to use the taut barbed wire fence topping as a means to launch themselves to the other side. Escapes now occurred every time the dogs were let loose outside. Valerie got a lot of exercise searching the neighborhood for her hounds at all hours of the day and night.

Because all three dogs were now spending an inordinate amount of time outside chained to their dog houses, Valerie was a bit lonely; she brought home a fourth dog—a Boston Terrier she named R2-D2. Jaina became R2's favorite playmate, and R2 was all about play. The clown of the pack, an unruly Tigger, R2 instigated play with whoever was around—humans, dogs, horses, anybody.

Thankfully, R2 couldn't jump over the fence, but he was a snitch. When he failed attempts to follow the others over the fence, R2 ran like a racehorse with a burr under its saddle to fetch Valerie and show her the exact spot where the hounds—who by now could have been Ringling Brothers' stars—had vaulted. However, even before he was completely house-broken (that took a couple of days), wily R2 revealed his own escape specialty—he deftly opened the sliding glass door to let the hounds out of the house.

Soon after R2's arrival, two police officers showed up at Valerie's house at 3:00 a.m. "We've had similar reports from three of your neighbors that you were wandering through the neighborhood a while ago and calling for Star Wars characters. Are you under any kind of mental health treatment?" The larger of the two policemen tapped his foot, his hand on his weapon. He stared at Valerie's frazzled hair and sweatpants covered in sandspurs.

Valerie invited them in and introduced them to the dogs—all four exhausted from their early morning romp and looking innocent as though they had never left. The cops left a few minutes later, one shaking his head as if to say, "I gave up my morning coffee for *this?*"

The next morning, Julie came by.

Valerie gave her a cup of coffee, related the night's events, and bemoaned the dogs' shenanigans and the nine pages of complaints logged by Animal Control as the result of as many calls from Mrs. Busybody. Valerie paced over to the sliding glass door and gazed out. She shook her head. "Barbed wire, cinderblock fortification, a tall fence—this exercise yard can lock down Leavenworth inmates, but not my damn hounds, the sons-of-bitches."

Julie set her cup on the end table. "You need to be grateful for those critters. They really are your best friends. It seems to me that since they've been here to distract you, you haven't had much time to think about losing your husband."

Valerie paused, glanced at her canine crew, and then nodded. "You know, you're right about that."

Just then, all four dogs tore past them and escaped out the back door. Black streak, tan streak, yellow streak, small streak—zoom, gone.

"Vader! Get back here!"

#

Peggy Insula, retired psychotherapist and educator, is a sometimes humorist who wrote "A Woman's Best Friend." Other publications include anthologies: *Pearls, Vain Imaginings,* and *Where Am I Going?* and longer works: *Murder Runs in My Family, Sudsy, Just Murder, You're No Body 'Til Somebody Kills You,* and *How Not to Steal a Car.* Insula's poetry appeared in *Metaphor.* Other works found places in the Brevard Scribblers' anthology, *Driftwood.,* and in Word Weavers' International blog.

MAGNOLIA SYMPHONY:
A STORY OF FRIENDSHIP

By Betty Jackson

I like to think of my life as part of a symphony orchestra, under the direction of the Conductor of the Universe, my Heavenly Father who creates all things, sustains all things, and Who writes the score, beginning to end, developing the melodies and harmonies into grand themes, and guiding the orchestration of my life's symphony to His Glory and Honor.

When He looks at this great composition, his masterpiece, He notices even me, this one soul at this moment in time. I'm seated at the piano, practiced and ready, my line is at the bottom of the score before Him; and, according to the grace of His Presence, I can at once be the soloist in a concerto, or the background accompaniment, or the percussive crescendo, or the silent observer at rest, merely counting measures until the glissando is needed. It is the Conductor who knows the piece by heart, beginning, middle, and climactic ending. He has chosen me, with my fellow orchestra ensemble members for our appearance, in this very time and place.

Few experiences in life are as precious as friendships that weather storms and vicissitudes, binding women through laughter, tears, prayer, philosophies, and daily routines. I know and love such a group of incredibly strong, vibrant, yet vulnerable women.

I am part of the Praying Magnolias, a group that, like a symphony orchestra, plays life in this community. Like a good orchestra, its core group is constant, players who know each other intimately, who respect each other's talents and abilities, are responsible for high expectations of excellence, who work together to achieve harmony and beauty, and who create unbelievable experiences for others. Guest players enter and exit, each bringing local color and unique flavor, but the core is constant, accountable, and under the Conductor's baton.

Just as a good symphony orchestra has a sense of continuity, The Praying Magnolias has a base, a history, and traditional foundation. In this case, Tonia, Sherry, Janice, and Becky began meeting together weekly for breakfast, prayer time, and accountability thirty years ago. They had young families then, trying to balance home, husbands, in-laws, parents, day-to-day routines, and lived their lives under God's guidance. They brought individual concerns, each showing her talents and interests, each finding affirmation in making life-music together. And they recognized that, "A day hemmed in prayer is less likely to unravel." (*God's Little Instruction Book for Teachers.* Colorado Springs: Honor Books. 1999, 2003.) They held each other accountable, praying for each other's needs, communicating often, worshipping together at Covenant Presbyterian Church in Palm Bay. How did they know what the future held, or what the Conductor's vision for them was? They were the players, the principals, so to speak, of the string section. The score, at least for them, had not yet been revealed. But they were ready for the Conductor's direction, and became the beginning of a soaring symphony.

For some thirty years, these lovely ladies have blessed each others' lives with friendship, have served each other as prayer warriors, have encouraged each other with their knowledge and insight, have been surrogate mothers to each other's' children, have met together weekly for early morning breakfasts, have commiserated through the hard times, have enlightened with medical and psychological information, have catered each other's kids weddings and events, and have held each other's faith walks accountable.

Each has shared, like players in a great symphony orchestra, unique perspectives, each has often spontaneously volunteered considerable talents to help in countless crises, and each has contributed to the strength of the group as a whole, like preparing for a great symphonic performance

I knew about this group when I lived in Florida the first time, from 1987 to 1997. I knew many of these sweet women as friends, then. We were all busy caring for families, raising children, involved with the busyness that surrounds active young women trying to be nurturers, career women, loving wives, tolerant and respectful daughters-in-law, and vibrant Christians in our daily lives.

I was teaching full time in other parts of the county, away from Palm Bay, where this group has centered on Covenant Presbyterian Church. These sweet ladies adopted me when I could be part of the group, but I was a mere leitmotif, listening in around the edges.

Then I moved to Iowa for ten years, and lost touch with most of these fine women. But, like a symphony, themes move in and out, motifs appear and disappear, and climaxes occur, adding to the richness of their story. When I retired here in 2007, I felt as if I'd never been away. The strains of music were still being played, the themes were engaging, and I picked up the song quickly. And the last movement is still being written.

I see this group as a fine symphony orchestra. The principal players, provide the foundation for what is to come. Before the first meeting, the first rehearsal, they study the music, insert bowings, mark the scores, and set the agenda, so the string section is prepared to play in unison. Magnolias bring ideas and more to share each week. Everyone knows that sometimes the violins, take center stage. Then, with the give and take, the flow of the lines, the violins back off and the violas shine. The sonorous basses abide by the rules, provide the tonic chords, the absolutes. Then the cellos swell with lilting melodies to bring the soul a voice. Together, the section interprets the symphony as the Conductor shares the vision with them. It is intimate. It is amazing as He brings abundant life, creates tonal color and memorable moments.

Others became part of the group, weaving their stories and their textures into the ensemble. In their times of coming together over breakfast, their rehearsal, so to speak, they discovered each other's talents and abilities, their individual gifts, and share their life stories and struggles.

The woodwinds enter. They provide local color, so to speak. The flutes bring joy, embellishing the themes. The wailing oboe or haunting bassoon add sonority, as if to remind that life has dark moments when all the soul can do is sigh. The clarinets add distinct flavor to the themes, and together the section provides rhythmic accents and subtle tones of constancy. Each voice is heard breaking into the harmony of the spheres, and much would be missed without such unique voices.

Themes expand, and just like in a piece of music, harmonies sometimes express discord and disorder which ultimately resolve themselves into the rhythm and constancy the group enjoys most. Just so, when special prayer requests surface because hard decisions are being made, or there's a sick child, or parents are divorcing, or a housing crisis emerges, the collective group deals with the issue. One friend will offer advice, another will tug and pull at that idea to assert a different theme, and someone else will show empathy, a cello line of beauty amidst the cacophony. They discover as a group, that "Friendship improves happiness and abates misery by doubling our joy and dividing our grief" (Ibid).

One mom proudly announces her daughter is the lead in the school play. Another brags that her son's basketball team is going to State. Another announces her hubby's promotion, along with the news that he will be traveling more and she'll be primary caregiver five days a week. And the quiet one, the one with no children home of her own, now has two foster children who have been dropped on her doorstep, sullen and unresponsive, or the one whose stepchildren are now handed over to hubby. She admits she needs help.

The brass section calls attention to itself, with tones of authority, with sweet melodies from the horns, and bombastic calls to attention by the trumpeters. The trombones, sometimes melodic, sometimes raucous, are the temperamental ones. They're changeable, unpredictable, with harmony or with staccato accentuation of a motif that will not, cannot be ignored. And the steady tuba moves like a leviathan through deep waters, substantive and strong, making the rules and speaking the truth.

Each movement of the symphony has its own character. When a group like the Praying Magnolias begins to gel, when its core group expands and other join it, there is a time of introduction and exploration of the themes, a stating and restating of purpose, a melody that keeps returning. That melody is acceptance, an understanding that anything said within the group is sacred, to be kept and cherished, to be shared only among its members, so that it is a safe place to express thoughts and difficulties. Themes work themselves in and out of the conversations. Gripes and discouragements in minor keys sometimes weave into the day's talk.

The percussion section is the workhorse behind the scenes, the foundation, the constancy, the continuo, the individualistic color which enters and exits, momentary flashes, unique perspectives whether bell-like or rat-a-tat, and vigorously, all-hands-on-deck, full throttle presence at the climax. I, sitting at my piano, am part of this section, awaiting my cue, following the score, ready at a moment's notice.

And so it functions, complete and whole, the symphony of controlled melody and its support system, with its crescendos and diminuendos, its combinations of leitmotifs, cadenzas, and themes, and ultimately its long-awaited climaxes, when, in perspective, it all makes sense. Each movement of the symphony becomes part of the whole, and in its entirety, speaks volumes by touching the soul of the audience and players alike. There is no feeling akin to musicians' "high" when it all comes together in brilliance, and each one knows the performance exceeds expectations.

Hard work, practice. We don our work clothes to scrub houses before or after they're sold, to plant gardens, to wash windows, to clean our attics, to prepare garage sales, to provide respite for an exhausted caregiver. Practicing charity and coming alongside hurting people is like aa cellist working out alternate fingerings for a marathon difficult passage or working our percussion assignments when the crowded stage prevents access. Much work exists and it must be accomplished through hard work, sweat, and sometimes tears.

Each one knows the others are praying that the situation will be resolved, and each pledges support to the others. One is an expert at childcare. One sister's forte is her treasury of diet tips and alternative medicinal cures for whatever ails another. Several are autism experts. Someone will become "other mother" and babysit little ones until the crisis is resolved. Another knows just what to do to solve an impending real estate disaster. Like a symphony, each comes alongside to play her role to the betterment of the entire group. And the friendships deepen.

When finances are tight and mom is home with three little ones with a tummy bug, and the puppy isn't housebroken yet, and the car-on-its-last-legs breaks down, and the bills are overdue, negative notes enter. Friends take up the theme, offer to bring chicken noodle soup that's already made in the freezer for just such an occasion; another friend who lives nearby walks the dog three times a day until the critter learns what weeds are for; and the clever-with his-hands husband diagnoses and fixes the car. When burdens are shared, friendships deepen, prayers are answered, sometimes miraculously, and the leitmotif resolves into a major key.

New friends join the group. The second movement begins. This is the age where the little ones are now in middle school and high school, and the little problems could become bigger, widening horizons can be scary and moms are close to losing their wits at becoming the sandwich generation. At once they're coping with adolescents and aging parents, and they're caught in between. While hoping their children are becoming more independent, the scherzo stage of the symphony begins. This is the frantic helter-skelter, the tug and pull of helicopter parent or tough love. The underlying desperate hope that each day's crisis is manageable. This is when the drums roll loudly, the trumpets blast, the bassoons moan, and the sweet string melody is indistinct. The Conductor knows it will all end to His glory. But the players don't know that yet. Eventually, the beautiful moments occur, and they seem miraculous. That's what each of these women shares when they get together. The question is asked at breakfast, "What was the highlight of this week?"

All of a sudden, it's time for graduation, college plans, romances, and "hoping I've done it right" moments when the family car leaves the driveway and only prayer preserves mom's sanity. Heidi Quade says, "A coincidence is a small miracle where God chose to remain anonymous I call them Godincidences. No one's arrested, no dents in the car, kids' psyches seem to be intact, and each one of the moms helps another with the graduation parties and shopping for dorm rooms. When life events are shared, the load lightens considerably, and this group of women includes some awesome problem solvers and party planners.

I'm the first one here today. I pick up the rolled silverware, greet our usual server, Denise, and another early Tuesday begins at the local Cracker Barrel. Today we're expecting about seven. Tonia's out of town, Becky has company, Sherry's preparing for a concert and protecting her voice from colds and flu and just plain overuse; Rebecca's cuddling grandbaby number three; and Paula's teaching at CCS. This is a typical Tuesday at 6:30.

I recently read, "Friendship improves happiness and abates misery by doubling our joy and dividing our grief" (Ibid). That's only part of the history of this group. Around this table, we share everything, and what we share we keep to ourselves so that we can be real with each other. We can disagree vehemently; we can discuss any possible topic; no one's feelings are discounted or belittled; and we know that as friends, we temper everything with love. The part I like best is that we pray together, and have found specific answers to prayer as a result.

But, we don't merely pray. During the last three weeks, we have served two recent widows by providing a funeral service luncheon, (yes, we've reached that stage of life), we have fed families in town for both of these funerals, we have housed guests, picked up people at the airport, run errands, also accompanied people to doctor's visits and chemotherapy treatments, attended and reported on political rallies and town meetings, bought baby gifts for new grandbabies born to these grandmas (yes, it's time for that now too), and taken numerous meals to shut-ins and folks recovering from surgeries. In other words, these ladies are ministering to others, not merely talking

81

and sharing ideas.

And what a diverse group it is. We have experts on decorating, running businesses, education, medicine, healthy eating, exercise, autism, child care, end-of-life issues, shopping, entertainment, the Scriptures, politics, gardening, GMOs, alternative medicine, real estate, etc. Yes, we're learning the ins and outs of technology we're too embarrassed to ask our kids to teach us. The conversations are stream-of-consciousness, and we never run out of ideas to share.

We come to the table with bags full of stuff for show-and-tell. "Look at this shirt I found at the thrift shop for five bucks!" one will gloat. Another has a recipe to share. Another, an article of the terrors of using sugar. "It feeds cancer, you know!" I usually have my latest book cover to get opinions on: color, lettering, the picture, the title, etc. And there are paint chips, and pictures of grandchildren, etc.

Now we tend to talk about what our kids and grandchildren are doing, what they're struggling with, the housing issues, the paying off student loans, the pregnancy struggles, how little ones are adjusting to school routines, where the best bargains are, and whose husband is considering retirement now. It's like déjà vu all over again. Thirty years ago, these young mothers discussed bedtime routines, potty training, how to support and encourage husbands, whether to work outside the home, furnishing homes with beauty and serviceability on tight budgets, homeschooling versus public schooling, or whether the fledgling Christian school at church would work, and the day-to-day struggles of young family life.

Now, the conversations turn to Social Security, end-of-life issues for the sandwich generation caring for kids and parents, get-away trips, when to retire, downsizing, and kids' promotions and finding their niches in the workplace. Among us, we have family members we pray for all over the world. And some of our former "members" are living far away from us, but still stay in touch electronically. And what a joy it is when some of our friends come back for a visit. They sit at the round table at Cracker Barrel and it's as if they never transferred to Atlanta, Phoenix, Chattanooga, or Romania. And

82

somehow, we all know the grandchildren's names, remember when kids performed together in the church play, and reminisce about the numerous wedding receptions, graduation parties, and baby showers we've hosted for most of them.

All these themes rise and fall, crescendos and diminuendos, as the weeks pass. Each woman knows the others value her. Each knows the handclasp or the hug on Sunday morning or Tuesday at breakfast, and each looks for signs of God's grace to keep them going until the next time they're together.

Faces around the table begin to change. Opinions are shared about each one's hair color, trying to ignore changes of aging. Mid-life crises emerge. New people are brought in; others now have jobs or careers that loosen the morning connections, but now are remotely attached. We learn from our kids to use cell phones and instant messaging, then teach each other. We carry iPads and phones smarter than we are wherever we go. We get "group messages" or texts or emails, and feel connected, even though we're not in each other's physical space so much. Lives become temporarily scattered.

Most of these amazing women are now part of the sandwich generation, between kids and elderly parents, and find their lives in turmoil. Many are experiencing that sandwich generational phenomenon with its emotional and financial implications—the role reversal that comes with parenting grown children and their parents or loved ones who are advanced in years.

Trips to funerals for grandparents, even parents, begin to occur. Making end-of-life decisions about assisted living or doctor's appoints become the trombones' themes, or the somber bassoons' cadence. Hubbies' travels and meeting airline schedules takes balance and commitment, and the house that's been adequate all these years, suddenly needs renovation. At a moment's notice, chaos can intervene, and the percussive gong and thunderous tympani get our attention. Life seems to be…a mess right now.

Several now are grieving the loss of our parents, or even siblings, but many are in the position of making end-of-life provisions for relatives in various stages of struggles. Now, even husbands. It is amazing to see the compassion and wise counsel from those who've already tread these slippery slopes, advising those in the trenches, so to speak. All of a sudden, we have two widows. This is new ground for us, and gives us pause, and just a little terror.

That's when being a Praying Magnolia finds its finest expression. These loving women can make any moment serene, with a, "I'll be in Orlando tomorrow. What time is his flight?" to "Let me bring dinner tonight. I have a roast in the oven," or "I used this contractor, and believe me, he's the best there is. Come see what he did in my kitchen!" And when the crying fits at menopause start occurring, these friends understand. Remember, anything said at the table stays at the table? This is when a friend is truly a friend, and the third movement of the symphony tells you it's going to be all right, eventually. For each one knows grace with a capital G and mercy with a capital M. Prayers are answered, and all is forgiven. Or as one has wonderfully put it, just like a mellow clarinet or soaring saxophone line emerging from the very heart of the orchestra, the woodwind section, "Real friends are those who, when you've made a fool of yourself, don't feel you've done a permanent job!" (Ibid). There's forgiveness at the cross; there's forgiveness among friends around the table at Cracker Barrel too.

Now college graduation and weddings take center stage. Soon there are grandchildren. Oh, the weddings and baby showers we've thrown for each other. These are the symphony "folk songs" sections, with rollicking dances, about the drudgery of decorating and un-decorating, and washing the pots and pans. Weddings are hard work, we've discovered. And there are tears as we realize or think falsely, that our parenting days are over. Not so! The topics of conversation have to do with the heartbreak of our kids moving away, or being so centered on their lives that they forget to call. There's rivalry and a little jealousy when the in-laws steal "our" kids, especially at holidays. And this is the time when husbands or we are retiring, when cruises begin, when extended vacations draw each other away from the scene, and when life gets complicated. In the symphony, this is when all the themes start to merge, and nothing is quite as distinct as in the first movement when the story begins. There's a little tension. There's a little uncertainty. And sometimes, there's a fleeting moment of cacophony, or depression, or entrance of some random unresolved melodic fragments.

The mutual understanding that God works in mysterious ways his wonders to perform is recognized, celebrated, and brought to the table. It edifies each one's walk with the true Conductor in charge of this symphony called Life. It is understood that there is no luck, but providence; there are no coincidences, but Godincidences! If we are walking with the Lord, He makes opportunities for us to witness, builds hedges of protection around us, and provides for our every need—those expressed, and those we don't even acknowledge.

We laugh together, oh my, how we laugh together. Some are mere smiles, some are chuckles over ironies, but some are belly laughs of pure hilarity. But more importantly, are the inner joyful utterances and ecstatic understandings of God's solutions to problems we each thought were impossibilities. Especially lately, as health issues compound, God's handiwork and perfect timing bring that special peace that passes all understanding to the fore. There is actual rejoicing when what others would consider coincidences once again lead to the phrase, "It's a God thing!"

These women are knowledgeable and involved in the affairs of the world. We are at the forefront of the abortion-prevention campaign that continues on a daily basis. We are politically active. We follow educational policy and local campaigns. We are news savvy and see the ramifications of misled policies and programs. We're not gripers, but doers. We, unlike the critics who just complain, take up the mantle and actually get involved to oppose injustice and change situations.

When elections fail to produce desired changes, we opt for the Biblical principle to pray for our leaders that God's sovereign will can be evidenced for His ultimate benefit. We pray for revival, work toward peace and prosperity, and await the Lord's direction in every circumstance.

Who knows how many sacrificial meals we have prepared. Those home from the hospital, or having house-guests, or the church-wide missions-week meal celebrate the culinary skills of this group.

We fill the cancer-fighter's home with delicious meals every other day for months, so Mom can concentrate on the chronic disease ravaging her body, and know that those along side are meeting her responsibilities. The bounty from our kitchens blesses untallied tables, and throughout the years has been substantial. Where there's a need, these Christian sisters step up and fill it, literally. And, I might add, with aplomb and willing spirits.

And so, this group of twenty-five or so women, now spread to other states and even other countries, some still area residents, some not, remains. We are in a far different place than we were thirty years ago. The final movement is not over yet, but we feel it closing in. Our parents are aged or gone, our kids have homes of their own, our careers are winding down, our health concerns are elevated, our homes are too big and it's time to downsize, to shed a lifetime of excess stuff, and yes, although sudden, and shocking, and "it can't be," we have our first and second dear ones who are recent widows. It causes pause. It's time for reflection.

We talk about writing our own memorial services. We are stressed over each doctor's visit for our spouses or for ourselves. There's a sense of unease. Retirement isn't easy. Tensions arise when husbands are home all the time, changing our routines, affecting our decision-making, and all of a sudden, we see dear Nancy, who would give anything to have more days with her Ray, and Tempa who has just said goodbye to her Tom. Yes, the close of the symphony is coming. Will it be triumphant? Will the themes be comforting? Will the minor key take over?

I think not. These talented and awesome women are conquerors because they realize their strength comes, not from themselves, but from their lifelong walks with the Lord. He guides. He strengthens. He comforts. It is His joy to celebrate the victories, to remind us of the days and years of His faithfulness, and He helps us remember that He holds the ultimate story and knows our role in it, from the very beginning of time to the present, and to the future.

So, our symphony continues. We will serve luncheons at each other's memorial services. We will accompany one another to doctors' visits so we can remember all the details. Yes, we need advocates now. We're having senior moments. We're hoping it's not the dreaded diagnosis of Alzheimer's. We will pray more. We are prayer warriors for all the hurt ones. We send more sympathy cards and plant memory trees. We will try the new recipes, exercises, medicines, alternative doctors' opinions to keep our bodies functioning. We will go to films and concerts together to give us highlights each week to look forward to, we will search the internet and Pinterest for the newest old thing, we will take vacations and come back, knowing home is best, we will tell each other tales of our grandchildren and even our great-grandchildren. We applaud our legacy of love and concern for our world, for Christ's kingdom, and for each other.

How did the title come about, The Praying Magnolias? I think the magnolia image says it all. Picture it as the tree it is. Strong branched trunks, yet delicate, support its closely linked limbs. From it, clusters of shiny leaves extend heavenward. They are brown underneath, which perhaps symbolizes the darker sides of lives through which friends give their unconditional love and advice, and vivid shiny green on the surface, which creates a sense of openness to life, and provides broad surfaces to take in the sun's warmth, the gentle rains, and even hurricanes' fury with few complaints.

And then, the magnificent flowers extend their purity, their beauty, their radiance, and their fragrance. Gorgeous, yet vulnerable, they shine for a season, then fade to let other blooms take center stage. Together, they provide a networked edifice of creation, structured much like this group of women, in their engagement in the whole.

The magnolia has long been known as a symbol of southern

strength, beauty, and love of nature. What a tremendous parallel this is to this group of fine women. Other traits often mentioned in connection to the magnolia are perseverance, because it is evergreen and long-lived, the trinity because of its clusters of leaves, sturdiness because it withstands disease, storms, bright sunlight, and harsh conditions, and health and healing since even its bark is used in medicinal preparations.

And who can forget, once having smelled its lovely flowers, the pervading fragrance which lingers, much like a lady's perfume, reminding of her presence even when she is far away. So it is with this bonded group of ladies.

And so it functions, complete and whole, the symphony of controlled melody and its support system, with its crescendos and diminuendos, its combinations of leitmotifs, cadenzas, and themes, and ultimately its long-awaited climaxes, when, in perspective, it all makes sense. Each movement of the symphony becomes part of the whole, and in its entirety, speaks volumes by touching the soul of the audience and players alike. There is no feeling akin to musicians' "high" when it all comes together in brilliance, and each one knows the final performance exceeds every possible expectation.

So may it be said that The Praying Magnolias symbolize the best that friendship has to offer. And may we perform our symbolic symphony as we live our lives individually and collectively, each playing a part, each gracefully providing melody and harmony, and each under the direction of the Lord we serve, the ultimate Conductor of all things beautiful in this world, in this very time and place. Amen So Be It.

# # #

Betty Whitaker Jackson writes Christian fiction, nonfiction, poetry, and devotional guides. A career language arts teacher, she has retired to Palm Bay, Florida where she now concentrates on writing. In the last four years she has published ten books, blogs regularly at https://www.bettyjackson.net and won First Prize in the LifeRich Reader's Digest Memoir Writing Contest. She is published in five anthologies and has a book trailer at https://www.youtube.com/watch?v=Pz_MPtVkiKY. She thanks SCWG for its encouragement.

FRIENDS BEGETS LIFELONG FRIENDSHIP

By Bob Konczynski

It was the summer of 1965, and I was to begin the first adventure of my life, a summer vacation not with family, but with a friend. After a period of time collecting brochures of various places to go from Atlantic City, Seaside Heights, Wildwood, all on New Jersey shore, to resorts in the Pocono Mountains of Pennsylvania, and after lengthy discussions, we chose to take a vacation in a small summer resort in the Kittatinny Mountain area of Northwestern New Jersey called Culvermere.

Not like today where you can gain information through the Internet, with personal reviews, we were off on an auto trip to an unknown place that was only described in a brochure as a summer vacation for singles. After a long drive leaving Staten Island, New York crossing the Goethals Bridge and entering New Jersey and following a paper map looking for US state roads and ultimately finding Route 206 a small winding road through the picturesque mountains of New Jersey we see a sign for Culvermere.

Upon approaching we were concerned as up on a hill was this old hotel and as we proceeded on to the grounds we saw a tennis court where one of the nets had a hole in it. First impression gave us this uneasy feeling; did we make a mistake in choosing this place for our vacation? It did not get any better as we were about to check in and was told that we were assigned to the bunkhouses in the rear of the hotel. Assigned room numbers and given the keys we proceeded to see what was the so called "Bunkhouse" and upon opening the door on the second floor we were surprised to see that the room was newly designed as if it were a room in Howard Johnson or Holiday Inn with two double beds and a private bathroom. After settling in with our luggage and portable bar we decided to make the best of it as good friends would do. There was a program guide as to the many activities that would be going on for the entire week and opportunities to engage in tennis, archery, horseback riding, sailing, canoeing and evening activities of dancing in a place called the cave. Meals were to be provided at different times for breakfast, lunch and dinner in the main dining hall.

The first activity was a get-acquaintance dance for all of the guests that were staying for the week. It was what I would call a multiple selection dance where it started out with the dance instructors beginning the dance with all of the guests gathering around in a circle and when the music stopped the dancing partners would change partners by choosing another person from the guests until all of the guests were on the dance floor. It must have been fate that during this dance that I was chosen by the most beautiful girl that I did see to dance with her. She was charming, her smile and friendly personality illuminated the room as if there was only the two of us dancing on the floor. We introduced ourselves and found that we were travelers from two different islands, she was from Long Island and I from Staten Island with quite a distance apart. Who could have imagine that within the next week full of exciting activities, with this new found person who was about to become my friend for life.

Photo by Bob Konczynski

After the get-acquaintance dance we had dinner and then it was off to the cave for dancing, drinking, and having a good time. So much of a good time that the next morning we missed breakfast and was looking for some type of breakfast snack and was told that there was coffee and pastries in the tavern room. So my friend and I went off to the tavern room where not only did we find coffee and pastries but we met that beautiful girl and her friend from the day before. They also missed breakfast and we gathered at a table and had coffee and read the funnies from the Sunday newspaper, shared jokes, and began to know one another better. An instant friendship was created and we went off together to participate in some of the activities of archery, volleyball, and then a relaxing afternoon on the lakefront beach.

As we participate in other things like horseback riding and canoeing we became closer and bonded our friendship. Especially when it came to trust, as this young woman threatened to tip over the canoe but did not. After a fun-filled week of sports, dancing, and conversation we exchanged phone numbers and parting with a friendly goodbye.

Photo by Bob Konczynski

After a week went by it took a bit of deliberation and quite amount of courage to make a phone call that changed my life forever. As my adventure began with the crossing the Goethals Bridge to New Jersey, I was about to cross another bridge the Verrazano-Narrows Bridge from Staten Island to Brooklyn to travel on the Brooklyn-Queens Expressway to the Long Island Expressway to meet my newfound friend. The bridge had just opened within the past ten months as if it were an omen of fate encouraging me to pursue a friendship with this enchanting girl.

The distance between our islands, from house to house, was about forty miles, going through city traffic and yet crossing another bridge the Kosciusko Bridge to continue my journey to Long Island. Our first date was going to the World's Fair in Queens, New York. Being late arriving at her home did not hamper the day and this sweet girl was very understanding and compassionate of my trip from Staten Island. The day was full of excitement and adventure as we visited many of the exhibits and explored the World's Fair. We ate at a modest restaurant and I can remember that we had a poor boy sandwich at the Polynesian pavilion and we had a wonderful time of joking, laughing, and some good conversation. The pleasantry of the day, her enchanting smile, gave a bonding of friendship that I had never encountered before.

There were many more trips from Staten Island to Long Island where our friendship grew to love and then marriage. It is now fifty years and we have had our good times and bad times but throughout the years our friendship has always flourished. If it were not for that vacation with a friend to Culvermere I would not have ever experienced this lifelong friendship with that beautiful, sweet, understanding, and compassionate girl who became my wife.

# # #

Bob Konczynski was born in Elm Park on Staten Island, NY. He met his love from Williston Park on Long Island, NY, married, and became a proud parent of three children and two grandchildren. He graduate from New York Institute of Technology with a Bachelor of Science degree. At a company request, he moved from Long Island, NY to Melbourne, FL in 1995, with multiple assignments to his current position of Sr. Financial Analysis at an aerospace company.

MY FRIEND FREDDY

By Robbie Konczynski

It's not often in life that a friend is given to you. However, it does happen, and this is the very thing that has happened to me when Freddy entered my life. Freddy was given to me on my very first birthday. His family origins are traced back to Fisher Price and he happily sports a red apple that is embroidered on his chest. Freddy has eyes of leather and is made of a very durable plush fabric. Except for a few tumbles in the washing machine he has survived my childhood and most of my adult life very well.

When one thinks of friends they don't normally think of a stuffed animal. Many times they think of people in their lives that have been brought into a close circle to the point where they are considered family members. Sometimes people think of pets and animals as being friends. I however, look at Freddy, who has always been in my life, as my friend.

My friend Freddy has celebrated every birthday with me. In fact, Freddy and I have the same birthday since he was given to me on my birthday. Every year Freddy and I both get excited when our birthday comes around. We wonder what gifts from other friends we might get. We wonder what special plans might have been arranged for us. We wonder if we will head out to Disney and have a nice day in the park or eat at a very lovely restaurant.

The thing with Freddy is that he has the same experiences as me. Freddy was with me when I graduated kindergarten. He was around for my sixth-grade graduation, my twelfth-grade graduation, and for my college graduation as well. I like to often think that Freddy has the same degrees I have because he has gone through the same trials and tribulations as I have done. My friend Freddy has stayed up late nights studying. He was there when I would have bad dreams of arriving to a test late. Speaking of dreams, Freddy is always there when I have good dreams and bad dreams. When startled awake from some awful dream, he is there to give me a hug and help turn on all the lights. Freddy has also had bad dreams and good dreams too. Sometimes Freddy's dreams are so bad I find him in the morning stuck between the wall and the mattress. When I find him that way I comfort him and tell him he must have had a wild dream to end up all the way over there. Freddy has also been sick. I know hacking up some stuffing must be hard for a stuffed animal but he comforts me when I have my issues too.

I never thought growing up that someday I would write about Freddy as my friend, but I realize it is the right thing to do since he is my oldest friend. Some of the examples of what makes Freddy a good friend are the following: Freddy always makes time for me. He always listens to my rants. Freddy is very patient and understanding with me too. When I complain about things he simply listens and he doesn't pass judgment. In fact Freddy is a very good listener and in part I think that is what makes him a great friend. When I am talking, not only does Freddy listen, he also doesn't interrupt me. Freddy doesn't give much advice but since he sits very patiently listening to me, I realize that this must be his trick and secret. Freddy lets me realize my own issues and that is why he gives such good advice.

When looking through old photos, one of the constants there is Freddy, my friend. Freddy has been to Hershey Park, Busch Gardens, NYC, the Adirondack Mountains, and pretty much all the places I have ever been. Once in a while Freddy would play hide and go seek and this would cause a panic for searching for him. Luckily for me, I was always able to find him, even if I needed some help.

Freddy has been my friend for as long as I can remember. Freddy is my pal, my buddy, and my friend.

#

Robert J. Konczynski, Jr. grew up in East Northport, NY. Robbie attended the Elwood school district and went on to the University of Central Florida for his Bachelors of Science in Computer Science, and then to Florida Institute of Technology where he earned his Masters of Science in Software Engineering. Robbie is passionate about technology, science, education, and model railroading. He currently lives in Melbourne, FL and is a member of Space Coast Writers' Guild.

WHAT IS FRIENDSHIP?

By Tracy Konczynski

How to answer the question of, what is friendship? Friendship can be defined in many different ways for many people. For myself, friendship can be defined in a simple matter that is not too complex.

Friendship is the *First* person I met, who gave me the First smile.

Friendship is the one who *Rushes* to your side and kisses the boo-boos away.

Friendship is the wise *Intellect* used to give advice, whether you want to hear it or not.

Friendship is the *Endearing* love that is given to you every day, through both the bad times and the good times.

Friendship is being a good *Negotiator*, knowing when to give and take, and making sure the things get done, when it needs to be done.

Friendship is having someone you can *Depend* on to be there through the ups and downs of life.

Friendship is the never ending *Support* that is given through the cheers, tears, and hugs.

Friendship is the *Helping* hand that always seems to be available whether it is a small or major crisis, and never questions.

Friendship is the *Incredible* understanding you receive, even in some cases when a decision wasn't the wisest one to choose.

Friendship is the *Patience* it takes to see one through their wins, losses, and problems, especially the earth shattering ones.

The definition of friendship means many things, and people may define it in many different ways. For myself, the definition of friendship is quite simple. Friendship equals my Mom.

# # #

Tracy Konczynski grew up on Long Island, New York. She graduated from SUNY Stony Brook University. She currently lives in Melbourne, Florida. Tracy is a Girl Scout Volunteer and enjoys the time she gets to spend with her sister and her niece's Girl Scout troop. She loves to read mysteries and enjoys crocheting. Most of all, she treasures the time she gets to spend with her family.

LETTERS

By Beth Lambdin

The phone rings. It is Carrie's father calling. I see his number on my caller ID and do not want to pick up the phone—but I feel kind of obligated, and it could be important. Carrie was my college roommate. But that was a long time ago; and in the years since, I've grown to not care much for the phone. It feels like an intrusion. I am turning into a member of Anne Tyler's Learys, the phone-phobic family in *The Accidental Tourist*.

I pick up. And it is important.

"Carrie is in the hospital," her father says. "She's having a bad reaction to chemotherapy."

Chemotherapy? I am floored. He says Carrie was diagnosed with breast cancer five months ago. She had a lumpectomy. Then they found cancer in six of her lymph nodes—and then the chemo started: two rounds. When that's done, she'll have a mastectomy and then radiation. Oh, my God.

"Any support from you would be great," her father says, adding, "She doesn't usually answer the phone."

Well, me either. What am I supposed to do? Send smoke signals?

How about letters? That I can do.

Just that, though. I'm tired. I'm worn out from being me. Lots of marriage angst and worry about my mother. I'm pretty sure she is in the early stages of Alzheimer's. My husband, Jim, isn't much emotional support when it comes to my parents. He's so self-contained that I want to poke him like a bear, with a big stick, just to get a reaction. I wonder what's simmering under the surface. He'll probably blow some day and murder me in my sleep. Hack me to death with a thousand blows.

After I hang up with Carrie's father, Jim comes home. I am obviously upset. I can barely get my words out, and he immediately gets that deer-in-the-headlights look. It enrages me. He can't handle my intensity. No move to hug me (although, honestly, I don't think I'd hug me either). Still, what is it with him? Is this reminding him of his father's cancer? His mother's? Who the hell knows?

Is Carrie going to die? She's only 47. *We're* only 47. My gut is going crazy.

Hi Carrie,

Your dad called to let me know how you're doing. And, well, this is a diagnosis no one wants to get. I am so sorry about this, and that you are having such a lousy reaction to the chemotherapy. You've had a rough time of it since April, that's for sure.

How are you feeling now?

It's a beautiful fall day here, today. We had violent storms and tornadoes Monday. The University of Maryland, my old backyard, was especially hard hit.

I went to an author talk last night. The author was talking about reading faces and auras. She did a mini-reading of my aura, and I found her to be eerily accurate. She focused on my heart chakra and said I have tremendous empathy. So now I'm reading about empaths.

I'll write again soon.

Love, Beth

Despite her father's comment about her antipathy to the telephone, Carrie calls me a week later. She sounds cryptic and vague. She's there, but not there. I don't ask her why she hasn't called over the past five months, and she doesn't say. You'd think almost thirty years of friendship would rate at least a note when she was diagnosed. But this is no time for recriminations.

After the call, I look up breast cancer and staging on the Internet and see that her five-year survival rate is 76%. I feel some relief. She's got a good chance to beat this.

I start a file and label it **Carrie**.

And I write again.

Dear Carrie,

How are you this week?

Did I tell you that I am in a children's book group? It's made up of four or us. The other three have elementary school-age children, so we've tended to pick books they can read with their kids. We're read "The Bad Beginning" by Lemony Snicket and "The Ant Bully" by John Nickle. I was wondering if your son, Sam, likes to read and what kind of stories he likes.

Jim left this morning for a two-day business trip to Florida. We've been having a tough time as a couple. Forces me to really practice program stuff. Until next time.

Love, Beth.

Bad dreams last night, something nipping at me. Woke up throwing off the covers, kicking at something invisible. Why didn't Carrie let me know what was going on? She got this news five months ago–*five months*. Couldn't she find a few minutes in all that time to pick up the damn phone and call? Why didn't she? She rarely calls, however, even under good circumstances. She just pops up now and then. We have a terrific time together and then she disappears for another few years. Sometimes, I seem to settle for crumbs when it comes to what my friends (and husband) are willing or able to give. Although, to be fair, Jim actually gives a lot in many ways.

Dear Carrie,

Happy Halloween! I'm assuming Sam is excited about the day. What's he dressing up as? Bet he'll be cute.

You are in my thoughts so much of the time. I watched a documentary on PBS last night called "Renee's Story," about a woman in her 30's who is battling Stage 4 breast cancer and underwent massive doses of chemo and some kind of stem cell procedure. By the end of the doc, she was cancer-free. She found the chemo to be the worst part of her treatment.

I'm wondering how your system is tolerating all this. I would imagine that the way to get through it is really program stuff, "one day at a time," a cliché, but a helpful one I hope, supplemented by mega doses of faith. I deliberately think of you in a healing way when I meditate and when I'm in church. I believe in the power of prayer. Did you ever think I'd be saying things like this?

Think I mentioned that Jim and I have been going through some tough times. A long story, but I had a "spiritual awakening" at a recent AA meeting, and it has made a difference in our relationship. At the meeting, a guy was talking about feeling connected. It was just what I needed to hear, as I spend much of my life feeling like I'm an alien from another planet. Then, after the meeting, I went out to lunch with a group from the meeting (very unusual for me) and had the most wonderful conversation with this woman about her 46-year marriage. She told me about her own spiritual awakening during a lunchtime conversation with a friend. That friend was talking about forgiving her daughter, and in that moment, my friend realized that was what she needed to do with her husband.

And, in that moment at lunch, I felt the Universe align for me, and I was able/willing to hear this message of forgiveness.

I want to tell you that I do not have any expectations about you writing back. As always I'd love to hear from you, but there is no obligation. My understanding of these treatments is that they can be extremely debilitating. My sole purpose in writing is to let you know I'm thinking of you and wishing you well. The last thing in the world I want to do is anything that provokes more anxiety. On that note, I'll end for now.

With love and great affection, Beth.

I say I don't have any expectations about hearing back from her, but is that true? Hearing nothing provokes my anxiety. Does she care if I write? Does she care at all? I haven't seen her in years–the last time at our wedding.

That day, all the people our age were sitting around one large table. Our friend, Nell, was regaling everyone with how she was responsible for Jim and me getting together, when Carrie came over to join us. There was no room for her at the table, and I said, "Hold on, we'll set another place and smoosh in for you." She said, "No, no, that's okay," and moved to the table where the older people were sitting. I have always felt bad about that, that there was no room for her at the young-people table.

Do I confuse history and loyalty with friendship? Carrie and I certainly have history. We made good roommates and were good friends, even if we weren't best friends. She was a go-with-the-flow kind of gal, blessed with a first-class temperament and elusive something just worked with us. We hung out. We watched *Love Story* at my grandmother's house down the street from the college, and sobbed so much that Uncle Tom was embarrassed for us and had to leave the room.

Once a friend, always a friend. Is that how it is?

Or do I feel I owe Carrie something? For what? Her support during the pregnancy? I got pregnant the summer before junior year. It had been such a fun summer, my boyfriend and I, in love and lust, hanging out together after work, sex on a scratchy blanket under the stars. And, then one night, the condom broke. We stared at its remnants, mutely, but neither of us felt real alarm–then. A few weeks later, I returned to school, and he left the country, unreachable for months.

No period in August or September and then I worried, really worried, and then I took a pregnancy test–and I was too nervous to call for the results, so Carrie did it for me. When I saw her face, I knew the results were positive. I felt anything but positive. I felt like I had done something really bad and now my life was over and I had no way to reach my boyfriend and was only getting the occasional post card from him written in his chicken-scratch scrawl. It was a lousy time.

Within a few days, Carrie and I drove my green, Chrysler Newport to S.E. D.C., to a clinic. When we got there, none of the girls and the women in the waiting room would look at me. We all stared at our feet. The procedure was short, but the doctor said, "Why did you wait so long?" and I felt such shame. I don't think that shame and guilt has ever left my body.

Hi Carrie,

Wondering how your last chemo went and how you are feeling. Hope that you won't feel too debilitated from this latest round.

I'm practicing "first things first" this morning. I've been feeling pretty scattered for the last couple of weeks and have a lot of stuff going on in my head about what I SHOULD be doing. So, the first thing I decided to do was write to you, and then I'll figure out what's next.

Had a busy weekend. My mother-in-law was honored at her church for her extraordinary service to the community. There was a formal presentation during the service, and then all of us family members went up front and read from a text written by Jim's sisters. It was quite moving. Of course, I could barely say my part because it had to do with her being a ten-year breast cancer survivor, and my feelings are so on the surface right now for you and your battle with the disease.

Having a kid, I imagine you've seen Shrek. *Jim and I rented it last Friday and really, really enjoyed it. Did you like it?*

Have you and Sam read the Harry Potter books? I read the first one for my children's book group and have been reading the subsequent books after Jim expressed some interest in them. I think they're good, not great, but whatever gets kids reading is a good thing.

I'd be happy to come stay and help out either after you've had surgery or when you're going through radiation. From what I hear talking to others, it's helpful to have a lot of support. My sponsor said that when she was going through breast cancer she didn't do anything alone.

Love, Beth.

Why did I offer to come and stay? It'd be terrifically disruptive on my end and I don't really want to do it, so why did I offer? Am I saying things because I think I should? Probably. What does the "Instruction Book for Friends of Friends with Cancer," say? 1. Offer support. 2. Call. 3. Write. 4. Go there. 5. Worry. 6. Put your own oxygen mask on first. 7. Don't sleep — toss and turn, instead. 8. Worry. 9. List all the ways you're failing to support your friend.

But what am I fretting about? If past behavior is an indicator of future behavior, like Dr. Phil says, she'll just never respond.

Not much support on the home front. Jim has been either

unwilling or unable to talk with me about her cancer (or maybe he's setting a decent boundary for himself). I know it isn't that he doesn't feel, and I know he loves me, but he's so kind of one note–no highs and no lows–it makes me nuts.

Or maybe I feel enough for both of us.

Why does that make me so mad? Am I actually angry at Carrie for not responding to my letters and putting that on Jim? Seems kind of superficial but not out of the question. Still, maybe I have more anger towards Carrie than I am aware of–for her silence over the years. But I can't get mad at her now because she has cancer and a young son and may die–so I get mad at my husband who is right here and not going anywhere.

We are going to Virginia Beach this weekend to the Association for Research and Enlightenment. I could sure use some enlightenment.

Dear Carrie,

How are you? I had a reading with a psychic in Virginia Beach. I've included the part that has to do with you. "J" stands for Joy, the psychic, and the "B" for me, of course.

Session with Joy

B: My college roommate is battling breast cancer right now.

J: Is she getting chemo?

B: She is.

J. Okay. All right. You know, she feels like she's fighting a tough battle. Which she may be able to win. I'm getting something about a second time. Is this a second time? Something about a second time.

B: She had a benign lump 15 years ago in the same breast where she now has cancer. She had a lumpectomy. I don't know if that's the second time or not.

J: That could be the second time. I'll tell you what, she's got a good chance of getting through this. She's going through a heck of a tough time with her life. Everything is converging on her but it'll be life changing for her. How old is she?

B: She just turned 47.

J: During this cycle, she's going to make tremendous changes in her life. She's already started, but she's going to make it. You know, I'll tell you, the Universe has a way of doing things – first they hit you in the head with a pebble, then a rock, and then they hit you with a brick. I think this gal can make it. She's got to absolutely hold steady to this. It's a test, test, test for her. She can do it. She can make it through this. The next couple of years are going to be amazing. She's going to recognize that she has a strength she never thought she had. I'm sure you'll be supportive of her. I feel like she has to work on this. I feel she has a good chance of making it. She's got to have a lot of support in her life. Okay?

I'm hoping that you find this interesting and comforting.

Hugs and kisses until the next time, Beth.

"*I'm sure you'll be supportive of her,*" the psychic said. *Any encouragement from you is great,* her dad said. Two adults telling me to be supportive. My Pavlovian response is to obey authority figures–and then to passively resist the hell out of them. Are my letters supportive enough? How about the time I spend worrying about her? Is that enough?

I am struck by how much emotional energy I'm devoting to Carrie–who has rarely even acknowledged my existence in the last twenty years.

Dear Carrie,

Hi, there. How are you? It's late morning here, and the sun is just beginning to show up after it being cloudy for the last few days. Nice to see it.

How was Thanksgiving? We had a very quiet time with just the two of us, and it was really nice. I love Thanksgiving. I feel a strong affinity for the day since being in recovery especially–I have so much to be grateful for.

We went to a 10:30 p.m. showing of Harry Potter the night before, so we were pretty wiped out, as we didn't get home until about 1:45 a.m. I feel like I can't give the movie a fair assessment because the sound was so loud I think my system shut down. It was beautiful to look at. But kind of lifeless. I'm finding that all the kids I've talked to so far really liked it, so there you go.

I'm getting increasingly dissatisfied with the tutoring I've been doing, but can't muster much energy for a job search, since I'm not sure, once again, what I want to do when I grow up.

Anyway, just wanted to let you know I'm thinking of you.

Love, Beth.

I've always settled for so little (Please sir, could I have a little more gruel?). I learned that from my mother. Sacrifice your needs and come second. Never, ever talk about your resentments, let them fester and then overreact to a "tiny" thing–a clumsy daughter breaks a gravy boat at Easter. World stops spinning on its axis as the mistress of the house runs sobbing from the kitchen. Daughter feels like shit–tries to mend the gravy boat, but it's beyond repair.

Same mother, now losing her mind. More stories coming from New York about her memory glitches–misplaced objects, a minor fender bender, a delusion that she's hit her hairdresser's car and fled the scene. Everyone around me needs so much care these days. Me, too.

Dear Carrie,

How are you? I'm wondering if you've had the mastectomy yet? If so, I hope it went well and you are home recovering. I imagine that Sam is excited about Christmas.

I'm kind of nervous about what I'm going to see with my mother when we go to New York next week. She's not in great shape, mental acuity-wise, and I want to be prepared for that. I also am hoping/praying that I am going to be able to stay detached in a loving way and not get as nutso as I usually do. It's a short visit, which should help. I wish they'd consider moving to a smaller, more manageable place, but suggestions about that seem to fall on deaf ears.

Jim left for Florida yesterday on a business trip to Cape Canaveral. Total solitude for a few days. What a gift!

That's about all the news from this end for now.

Love, Beth.

It's hard to feel the burdens of others so acutely. How do I keep my heart open and yet not sacrifice myself? And is Carrie ever going to write back? If not, how long do I keep writing to her? Until her father tells me I can stop?

I freaked at my recent ob-gyn appointment. My fear about the lump they discovered a few months ago put me on high alert. The mammogram was very uncomfortable, but after a few day of worry waiting for results, all is okay. Come back in a year. Relief! Paralyzing fear of the unknown turns me into a rigid ice sculpture. Now, I can melt back into human form.

Dear Carrie,

How are you progressing with recovering from the mastectomy? Any word yet on when you'll start radiation?

I've spent a lot of time since we've returned from New York thinking about my mother and reading more about Alzheimer's. But my father is still in denial. She needs to see a neurologist for a diagnosis and treatment plan. My biggest concern with their do-nothing policy is that they've lost valuable years when she could have been taking a medication that may have slowed the progression of the disease and improved the quality of their lives.

Been to the National Gallery three times in the last two weeks to see shows. When you're feeling better, it'd be great if you and Sam could come down, and we could see some of the sights together.

Gotta go, will write again soon.

Love, Beth

Does Carrie read my letters? And if she does, does she care about my mother, my father, my own fear of Alzheimer's? If she cared, wouldn't she respond? But I can't make my caring for Carrie dependent on hers for me. How could I not be kind to Carrie in her time of need? If I've got a pot full of gruel, I should share. Right?

Dear Carrie,

How are you? I'm hoping the radiation treatments aren't turning out to be too debilitating.

Well, our latest trip to Virginia Beach was unbelievable! Really life-changing in some ways. Jim and I both had individual psychic readings. And we heard that we have a VERY strong connection to each other and overall a good marriage. We are definitely in a rut and letting the problems define the marriage. Melinda (the psychic) gave good advice, like we need to be able to disagree with each other and feel okay about it, Jim needs to express his emotions and especially his anger and not shove it down, I need to stop trying to control him, etc. You catch her drift.

We were both able to hear these things from her and not get defensive. We haven't been able to do that in our own conversations. Good stuff! Bless you Melinda!

The neurologist has made a preliminary diagnosis of Alzheimer's disease for my mother but is reserving a final diagnosis until some test results come back.

When we walked into the workshop in Virginia Beach, here's what it said on the blackboard, "Remember to Surrender." Guess the Universe is trying to tell me something.

Love, Beth.

My desire to be kind is bumping up against being pissed that Carrie isn't acknowledging/responding to my letters (even though I told her it was okay not to). Here's a draft for her, if she wants to use it: *Hi Beth, I'm not feeling great, pretty wiped out in fact from all the treatments and barely holding on, but wanted to tell you thanks for writing. I love you, Carrie.*

Fat chance.

Dear Carrie,

How are you doing? I hope that the radiation treatments are not as awful as some of the other treatments you've endured over this past year. You've certainly had a hell of a year!

Jim and I went to hear John Waterman at National Geographic last night discussing his adventures kayaking the Northwest Passage. He was a very good speaker and particularly interesting talking about his interactions with the native Inuit people. He said they believe that the souls of their ancestors are present in their children, so they don't generally discipline the kids in any way (kind of hard to discipline one's grandmother).

He spoke of his deep love for solitude, communing with animals, surrendering to fear, the kind of profound stuff that said to me this man is on a spiritual quest.

My parents still haven't gotten the results of my mother's CAT scan, but she has started on Aricept, a move in the right direction. My mother said for the first time – to me, at least – that she believes that she has Alzheimer's Disease. Of course I'm profoundly sad about that, but am relieved they are taking action and moving out of denial.

Until next time.

Love, Beth.

I feel more and more like my words to Carrie are echoing into the void. What about that void? What's the void in me? Why is it terrifying?

Hi Carrie,

It's cloudy and cool here today, a perfect day to build a fire and stay inside with a good book. How are you? How is the radiation going? I do hope that you haven't been feeling too bad.

Is Sam getting excited about Easter? How's he doing?

My father said my mother seems significantly improved since taking Aricept. Apparently, she's been able to write checks again and is better oriented. Glad to hear that, but my sense is that this improvement is probably temporary.

Jim may be going down to Florida for an extended period in May. It all depends on whether his company is successful in winning this latest contract with NASA. Neither one of us is thrilled about the possibility, but we'll adjust and adapt.

Love, Beth

* * *

I continued to write to Carrie for another few months while she finished her treatments. My mother continued to have moments of clarity and even played bridge for a few more months before she started a precipitous decline and I became just some random, middle-aged woman with dirty-blonde hair (that my language-impaired mother called "black"), who visited from time-to-time. Jim continued to make frequent trips to Florida for work and the ache I felt from missing him was a potent reminder of how much I love this man.

Carrie did indeed survive breast cancer. And, after her father called to let me know she was out of the dark woods, I wrote her one more letter.

Dear Carrie,

Your illness has brought up so much in me: my abiding love and concern for you, of course, and my fear that you might die and that your young son would lose his mother, but also, my anxiety about how to respond, and my confusion about just what our friendship means.

I have been surprised at how much resentment I've felt when I didn't hear back from you. But, curiosity eventually replaced resentment, and I began to see a pattern playing out here. It looks like this: I pick a person: my mother, my husband, or a friend – and then expend an inordinate amount of energy caring about them. Mostly, this caring doesn't get external expression. Instead, it's an inside job. Worrisome thoughts and feelings and good intentions swirl around, accumulating more and more psychic weight until I am thoroughly worn out.

Patterns are mutable, though, and easier to change once we recognize them. Your lack of response helped me do just that – see that, once again, I was caught in a trap of my own making. I kept hoping you would respond, and give me the attention that I craved and believed would help me to feel good about myself. But, that wasn't your job. It never was your job. Your job was to take care of yourself. During your illness, you were doing exactly what you needed to do: focusing on getting well and caring for your family.

Finally, I see that we haven't had a "real" relationship, a friendship with mutual reciprocity, for many years. Upon hearing of your diagnosis, though, I spun myself into my own web of fatigue because it was a familiar way to react, one that I subconsciously hope will bring the reward of a matching level of appreciation. But, you did not respond to my invitation to participate. You held to your own ground, doing what you needed to do for yourself. And I learned from that.

So I end this letter with gratitude that you survived and will see your son grow up, and appreciation that I am now likelier to be more awake to my own ploys. I keep hearing a line of poetry whispering, "Don't go back to sleep." Who says, that? Rumi, I think. Wise words to heed, "Don't go back to sleep."

Love, Beth.

After printing this letter out, I set it on the corner of my desk where it sat and then sat some more, until dust started to collect on it. Finally, I tucked it into the file labeled **Carrie** – and there it remains unsent.

# # #

Beth Lambdin. is a non-fiction writer, essayist, memoirist and award-winning film critic. She reviewed films for *The Voice of the Hill, The Senior Beacon* and the *Washington Window.* She has been published in *The Washington Post, The Orlando Sentinel, The Leader Herald* and *Natural Awakenings.* She is currently working on a collection of personal essays. Beth lives in Cocoa Beach, Florida, with her husband, Jim, and their three cats: Cody, Cayce and The Great Catsby.

They Were Not Looking for a Friend

By Thomas Mayberry

Kim was a strict, no-nonsense manager who was determined to rise above her peers in her management career. She took her business very seriously and expected her staff to live up to those same tough standards. Being an aggressive, strict manager would definitely guarantee success and recognition. That is what is expected, in her mind, to get promoted. She had seen it numerous times throughout her many years in the food service industry. There was no one that was going to prevent it from happening. You could call it an obsession. She knew the names that she was called behind her back but it did not affect her.

The climb up the management levels within the previous organization was not going at the pace that she was willing to accept. Kim searched for a different company and was hired as the cafeteria manager at an employee cafeteria in the national headquarters for a major retail chain. Immediately she had her sights set on the next level up as the district manager. During the interview process, her new boss had promised her the promotion whenever the position came available. There was no guarantee how quickly this could happen. It may be a few years from now, or it could be in a few months.

He was a kind, caring man who was blessed with the talent for cooking and taking care of friends, family and customers. Jeff was also a cafeteria manager with the same company and had come on board a couple of years prior to Kim. He was also promised, by Daniel, the promotion to district manager, unbeknownst to Kim.

A few months later, Daniel was promoted and his position of district manager became available. Kim was awarded the role. As can be expected, Jeff resented his ex-boss for not promoting him as well as resenting Kim who was promoted. When Kim went to his cafeteria to survey the operation and work with Jeff on how to improve the business, she was not looking for a friend. This was business, strictly business. They were cordial, and nothing more. Over the years, she was so focused on moving up the leadership ranks in an organization that she tended to move from location to location and never took the time to get to know the staff very well. Why would this job be any different?

The company was growing quickly and adding more locations over the next few years. Kim was doing what she did best. She was building sales and profits. It was a rocky start for the relationship of these two opposite driven people. Kim felt that the company would be better off without Jeff because he was not cooperating with her initiatives and did not run his place like she would if it was hers. She was blind to his talents, and he could not disregard his resentment for her as his manager in the position that he was promised. The two of them tolerated each other, but nothing more.

As the years went on, they started being more open with each other about their feelings and how they got to where they were in their relationship. The more they shared, the more it started making sense. The grudges started to melt away. There was no longer the underlying battle going on. Kim ended up moving on to another department within the company and Jeff went off on his own to open up a catering business which grew into a small, thriving family style restaurant. He was doing what he loved. He was cooking and taking care of family, friends and customers. He was very successful. Kim was moving up the ranks and considered that a success as well.

They kept in touch even though they no longer worked together. There were not a lot of her peers that she associated with outside of work. She had always kept her business and personal lives separate. Jeff was no longer a fellow employee, so she let down her guard. Kim became friends with Jeff's whole family. Jeff was always involved in food through his catering and at his church. Kim helped her out when she could on the bigger events and got to know Jeff on a personal level as the years went on. There became a small circle of friends that used to work together that bonded as the years passed by. Catering events brought them together.

They shared the joyous times of their lives as well as the deepest pains. There were celebrations of the additions into the families and the mourning of loved ones that went to be with our Lord. Kim was not used to that, but deeply needed it. She had been so lonely over the years and had not even realized what she was missing out on. There was a void in her life that was being filled in.

Twenty years passed since Kim and Jeff first met through work. Neither one was looking for a friend out of the business relationship. When they look back, it just happened. They now consider each other one of their closest friends. Your tightest friendships are the ones that you do not have to put a lot of effort into. They just feel natural and develop on their own. Kim and Jeff now enjoy a very dear friendship even though they were never looking for a friend.

#

Thomas Mayberry. received his Bachelor's degree from the University of Northern Colorado in 1981. His passion is teaching people how to take their faith in God and use it in their personal and leadership roles. Thomas published his first book, *Faith Guided Leadership*, in 2011. All three of his books, including his most recent publication, *A Marathon Journey, Lessons in Goal Setting*, are available through Amazon.com. You can subscribe to his blog at http://faithguidedleadership.com.

AN UNEXPECTED DISPLAY OF FRIENDSHIP

By Ashley McGrath

During my senior year of high school, I wanted to attend the prom, but I didn't have a date. So, I asked two of my friends if they would accompany me, and they said yes.

Early in the evening on May 1, 2004, my friends came to my house, where we kicked off Prom Night with a Chinese dinner. Then, my mother (who served as a chaperone along with my father) drove us to the dance at the Maxwell C. King Center for the Performing Arts. The theme of the prom was "A Moment in Time." The dance hall was decorated with black and teal balloons and streamers, displaying school colors. Seated at a table covered by a white tablecloth, my friends and I drank punch, chatted with classmates, and danced during a few songs.

A couple of hours later, my friends and I heard it was time for the prom king and queen to be announced, so we went to the back of the dance hall. What happened next astounded me: I heard my name announced as the prom queen!

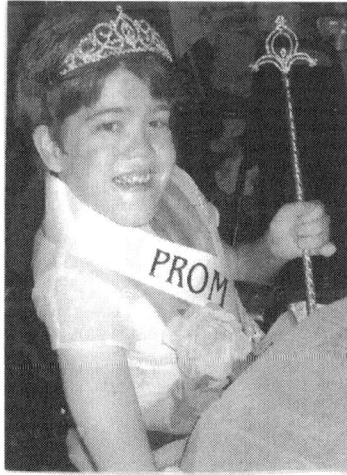

There was loud applause and cheering as my friends cleared a path for me through the crowd. The previous year's prom king presented me with a white sash that matched my dress, a tiara encrusted with cubic zirconia, and a silver foot-long wand matching my braces. The teacher who was our class sponsor gave me a bouquet of roses. Several of my classmates congratulated me; one of them said she voted for me twice! Following tradition, I danced with the prom king, a football player, for a song while all eyes were on us. This was truly a surreal "moment in time" for me.

Prom Night is unquestionably one of the most memorable nights of my life. Being crowned prom queen made me realize my classmates had a lot of respect for me regardless of my physical disabilities. I'll always be grateful to my high school friends for this touching gesture.

#

Ashley McGrath is a quality analyst for the call-monitoring company J.Lodge. Born and raised in Brevard County, Ashley has a master's degree in Applied Sociology from the University of Central Florida. She published her autobiography *UnabASHed by Disability* (which is available on Amazon and Kindle) in 2014. She was also a contributor to the Space Coast Writers' Guild's first three anthologies. Ashley is a SCWG Board member, motivational speaker, and volunteer.

THE BOND OF WARRIORS

By David Miller

The one that got away. Everyone's great fear in life. The one that got away.

Friendships come in all shapes and sizes. Friendships form under all sorts of circumstances. My own personal favorites are friendships formed from happiness. Family friendships tend to be enduring except when politics comes up at the Thanksgiving table. For that occasion, "enduring" means getting through the day. Friendships can mature from mutual trauma. On a grand scale, this type of friendship was created overnight for hundreds of millions of Americans who suddenly found themselves united after Pearl Harbor. Then there are friendships out of necessity. These are the worst for they are usually uneasy because that is not true friendship.

There is one brand of friendship that only a certain class of people can ever grasp. Those people are warriors. These warriors are as one because at some point in their life, they put their very existence on the line for the ideal of honor and country. Yet, it is not necessarily honor and country that welds them together. It is rather the bond of service. The bond of facing their duty and possible death is their glue. It is a super-glue that is almost impossible to explain to someone else.

Combat veterans certainly have the strongest warrior bond. They understand more than any other group of Americans, what it is like to squash fear because your friend is in trouble. They understand more than any other group, the friendship support needed when facing death. Even in battle, you never really get used to the idea of dying but rather you drive through that fear with your friends at your side. Just service to your country by itself is a strong bond. That shared fear of what your job entails whether it is pulling the trigger or supporting those who do, is a reward that few understand.

Warriors do not always understand nor agree with the politics of their conflict. They do their duty. The warriors who talk the least about their service are usually the warriors who went through the most. The reasons are simple. Those combat memories are not good so why relive them. No one would understand the depth of emotions involved other than a fellow warrior. Thus many spouses never know about what their warriors have been through. Sometimes thirty or forty years later they find out and finally understand those pensive moments that their warrior never talked to them about. Many marriages have decayed for all the wrong reasons.

Warriors will talk to other warriors about certain things but this also depends on the level of trauma of their experience. Someone who has experienced face-to-face combat. Someone who has felt the breath of a bullet just missing his face. Someone who felt the pain that comes with earning a Purple Heart. Someone who has left body parts behind in the war-zone. These warriors may feel uncomfortable around a warrior who has not experienced mortality this close and personal. So there are degrees of friendship and bonding within the warrior community.

The universal bond remains their service. This attribute is respected at almost all levels of the warrior community. Perhaps this is why few people can understand the intense pain to those who served, when people chose to publicly dishonor the American Flag as a means of protest. This is not the forum for such a protest. Regardless of the perceived injustice, protesters who use the American Flag are dancing on the graves of every veteran of every war. What they are protesting becomes insignificant to the insult they are perpetrating on all warriors, dead and alive. Warriors weep at such insults. Warriors become infuriated on behalf of their dead friends at such blatant displays of hate.

Yet these same warriors are the ones who fought for the rights of even idiots to do idiotic things. We live in a country that is governed by a multitudinous minutia of rules and regulations yet some among us applaud such hateful acts as free speech. The warrior cult should not be the only one that recognizes this truth. Yet this band of brothers seems to be the only group with clear vision on this matter.

Sometimes being a warrior can be quite painful yet the friendship endures.

There is another pain the warrior friendships must endure. Post Traumatic Stress Disorder (PTSD) strikes because of trauma. The bond of PTSD is not one that is normally "bragged" about. It is one that often is not even recognized by a warrior. Instead it lurks in the back of their brain whether the warrior is aware of it or not. It seems more prevalent among Vietnam combat veterans. The reasons are twofold. One, because of helicopter warfare, Vietnam warriors found themselves in actual combat more than four times as frequently as World War II vets. In Vietnam, the average days of combat in one year was two hundred forty days! Two, unlike World War II veterans, Vietnam veterans were almost universally rejected by their own citizens upon returning home. This was a sure formula for increased cases of PTSD.

PTSD is not confined to warriors. Any sufficient trauma will do. In fact, another class of "domestic warriors" known as police and firefighters are subject to stress disorders. It may seem like there is little to choose between the horrors experienced by first-respondents and those of combat. The differences however are quite monumental. The gore, the disgust, the pressure and the stress seem related but there two differences. The gore that first-responders see is usually perpetrated on people who are strangers to them. The gore that warriors see is that of their friends. The friends they fight with, eat with and live with every day. To this, add the daily constant fear of death and one can understand the emotional depth of combat related PTSD.

This mental disorder of PTSD is often unspoken. Many warriors deny its existent within themselves and are not that fond of comparing notes with other warriors. Unfortunately the treatment of PTSD requires talking about it. Among warriors there is only one possible way to accomplish this. Talk to other warriors. This works only because of the bond of warriors.

Pray for our warriors. Pray that they may experience a peaceful mind. Pray that they may get a good night's sleep far away from their hidden memories.

Pray for their friendship. Pray that they are not forgotten again.

# # #

David Miller is a U.S. Army combat veteran who served with the 188th Assault Helicopter Company in Vietnam. He is currently a Director at the Brevard Veterans Memorial Center and the newsletter editor for Vietnam and All Veterans of Brevard. He also serves as the Chairman of the City of Palm Bay Recreation Advisory Board. His books *90mph Door* is a true story of his life in the decade of the sixties. *Target Savannah* is based on a true incident involving an Air Force B-47 and a lost hydrogen bomb. Terrorists find the bomb, repair it and place it in a Saint Patrick's Day parade float.

REMEMBER ME?

By Ken Miller

How old were we, eight or ten? I don't remember, but after six decades the memories are still clear in my mind as if things had happened yesterday. It was a true and pure friendship, at least on my part. The tree house that he built in his back yard fifteen feet off the ground anchored in an old oak tree was the best I had ever seen. He cleared the canopy and added different levels that kept expanding into different rooms. Two ladders got you up there, a rope one, and a leaning one. They were both pulled up once we got there. The weather in the Bay Area was always cold and foggy with no mosquitos to worry about. Equipped with sleeping bags, the tree house was heaven for all the young kids in our group. There, we felt safe and talked mainly about sports and from time to time about girls until the night covered us with dark and we fell asleep, waking up with the sounds of nature.

Ray Holist was his name. Chubby and smart, he was a natural artist. "I am going to be an architect," I heard him saying more than once, as he kept drawing and planning additional rooms for the tree house. He never knew that years later I hired a person to build a tree house for my children, and fond memories of a time forever gone came back each time I saw it. Every time I reconnect with nature, the mornings waking up in Ray's tree house come back to mind with a sweet feeling.

We went to elementary school together. We both were "traffic boys," helping younger students to cross the streets, a job that is done now by adults and is called "crossing guards." We were trained to stop the flow of traffic for young pedestrians to cross school intersections. In that position we had a few privileges, including getting lower rates at the movie theater where we went every Saturday. The theater was full of kids running around, yelling and screaming while watching black and white movies. The Flash Gordon weekly episodes kept us coming back.

We took the bus from El Cerrito to Berkeley, a 45-minute ride, to see the University of California football games for a reduced fee, again due to our position as "Traffic Boys," and we were given a free frozen orange juice in a cup called Gremlin. Football games were fun regardless which team was playing. As soon as we got a chance, we played football on a field or in the backyard, always dreaming to become one of those famous players that we admired.

Our school was located in Berkeley too, so we were familiarized with that route. Back then it was safer than now for young kids to use public transportation. We walked to a few places. From my house down to the creek we walked to catch green frogs and pollywogs, while listening to Elvis Presley's songs on a battery operated transistor radio. Armed with a lantern, we shined the bright light directly into their eyes, which made it easier to catch them. We brought them home to have frog competitions, or placed them inside a circle to give freedom to the ones that jumped out of it. In the end, winners and losers, they all were released in our garden.

I remember a little park full of rocks in the Berkeley hills where we went to hang out. There was a cave that had been cemented, so kids couldn't get in. One day, we noticed that somebody had broken the cement, and full of excitement, we crawled down and got stuck. The fire department took us out of there.

We grew up and went to different high schools. Which teenager doesn't have a story of getting in trouble here and there? Like when our friend Pete drove Ray and I to a show. He had a driver's license and told us that he was going to Richmond to buy beers. "I look twenty-one, it always works," he said. He stopped at an old liquor store, got out of the car, but left it running. We saw him coming back with three six-packs of beer under his chin. "I got it, I got it," he shouted with excitement. Just as he sat in the car, a policeman pulled his police car behind us. Ray screamed: "Hit it, Pete!" Pete took off. The cop got back in his car and began chasing us. I said: "Are you crazy? Pull over." Once he stopped, the policeman got out of his car with his hand on his holster, and said: "Everybody put your hands up." Upon verifying that we were high school students, he asked,

"What are you guys doing? You are avoiding an officer. Who bought the beer?"

"Don't tell him anything, Pete!" Ray shouted.

"Okay, boys, you are in deep trouble. I want you to drive behind me very slowly. Follow me to the police department. Any bad movement will make your situation worse. If you try to get away, you will be prosecuted," the officer said in a voice that didn't leave room for doubts. Pete drove to the Richmond Police Department, and the three of us entered the interrogation room.

"Enough of this," the officer said. "Who bought the beer?

"I did," Pete said.

"You guys can go," said the interrogating officer. You need to tell your parents that we are going to call them."

"We were all involved in this," I said.

"Pete is going to get a $500 fine and lose his driver's license for six months," the officer said.

"I will talk to you later, Pete," I said, getting out of that room fast.

This was my first and last encounter with the police.

Ray and I had our moments of disagreements from time to time, but we figured out how to bring harmony back without applying lessons in conflict resolution, a concept that I learned later in life when managing adults.

Time, growing up, moving, finding new friends, cultivating different interests, and other circumstances kept us apart for years and years. Over forty years I tried occasionally to find Ray through Google, checking his high school alumni association, to no avail. Later on, Facebook came with all the possibilities of reconnecting with the past. Talking about the subject of finding friends during lunch time, a coworker suggested this venue. He entered Ray's name and the year he graduated from El Cerrito High School, and there was his picture, a gentleman as aged as I was, but the same smile. He was living in Canada. Right then, I wrote a note to let him know that I had not forgotten him, and that I had a desire to catch up. I left my phone number.

Two years have passed, and I continue waiting. He didn't show any interest. As painful as it was waiting for a response, I understand his decision. The perspective about how beautiful a friendship is or was can be different on each side. Evidently, on my side the moments were treasured. Nurturing is a two way street, and I was busy with my career and family and my efforts to find him were not strong enough. I have learned through life that in order to maintain any relationship including friendship, you have to invest energy, effort, and most importantly time. Hope is the last thing to lose. Therefore, I wouldn't be surprised if one of these days, Ray knocks at my door and asks, "Do you remember me?"

# # #

Ken Miller was an educator wearing different hats for 42.5 years: teacher, activities director, coach, vice-principal, principal, and superintendent in California. Even though he had written many school articles, business letters, employee evaluations, and other documents that could have amounted to more than one book, only after moving to Florida he was able to find time to become a non-fiction writer.

BLOOD SISTERS

By J.P. Osterman

(For Carolyn Clark)

"Jump, Carolyn! You can do it!" I called behind me, panting, as Carolyn and I ran alongside the jagged extension of slow-moving boxcars *clickety-clacketing* down the long railroad tracks toward Chicago. Distant, purple-gray corpuscular clouds unleashed a brisk warning wind, the bluster refreshing my face, arms, and legs— igniting me with a burst of energy. "Hurry! We don't have forever!" The oaks and spruce trees beyond the tracks had bending boughs, a sure prediction of a tornado warning. If we were going to pull off this stunt as planned, we didn't have much time left. "You can do it! I've almost got the rail!" The steel rod was blinding silver. "Almost— almost!"

"I'm—tryin', Joyce!" Her wobbling legs and scrawny arms flailing, she gasped, obviously straining to keep up with me.

This isn't like her. She can usually almost outrun me in track practice. Is something wrong? She just turned twelve, two weeks ago, after my birthday. Something didn't feel right, and I felt a change in the late-august air right then and there for Carolyn and me.

"You go on ahead, Joyce," she shouted and coughed through heaving breaths. She slowed down and then dropped back into the pebbly strand next to the tracks. She hunched down in fatigue like a chased cat desperate for air. "I can't—can't take another step— sorry!"

Letting go of the rail, I nearly fell on the rocks and flailed like a newborn deer gaining her first steps, until I quickly regained my balance. The train picked up speed, and we backed away from the intensifying noise for fear the boxcars' undertow might suck us into their shiny churning wheels. When we were safe at the border of Harrison Park, we stopped and watched our dream pass us by. "Darn! I thought we agreed we'd hop a boxcar for fun for turnin' twelve," I smoldered. "Shucks."

"Sorry, Joyce." Carolyn patted her hands on her stained beige shorts and tugged with disappointment on the hem of her lilac-flowered blouse. Wow, did dust hit the air! I had twice as much on me. "Anyways," she continued, "my ma will whoop me if she finds out we're anywhere *near* these tracks. I guess, I—I chickened out." She brushed back her short brown hair, and sweat glistened on her forehead, making her sea-green eyes beam like those luminescent fish we studied in the *Old Man and the Sea*. Waving lingering fine particles out of the air, I walked up to her to check and see if she was okay. Used to be, we were head-to-head in height. Suddenly, she was an inch shorter. Wow, did eatin' all June long sure make me grow like a string bean on a well-watered stalk! In the fast-rolling reflection of steel train wheels, I saw a dirty reflection of my face—blotchy sun-tanned cheeks with sun-bleached streaks in my pixy blond hair.

"You think *your* mom would spank *you* for hoppin' a train? Heck, a spanking is nothing!" I glanced at my dirty clothes. "My mom's going to whack me for sure with the broom handle when she sees *these* socks."

"Why would she do that?"

"She'll say, they're so filthy, they'll mess up the entire laundry load."

"Gosh darn!" Carolyn began patting my back to shake off some of the dust I'd accumulated from running into bases earlier in the day.

"Don't bother. It's no use. Between now and the time I get home, I'll have to figure out a way to get rid of some of this dirt or else I'm as good as rotten meat." Suddenly, I didn't care. Like the doctor once told me after a round of immunizations, I realized I'd become immune to all my mom's hollerin', and yellin', and smackin' me around...Crazy Mary.

The sun still high in the sky without the storm clouds yet blocking it out, I kicked a few pebbles as we walked down the cattail-lined path leading into Henderson Park. We were heading to the barn-shaped community building now open for business. I could hear kids laughing, obviously working on crafts and playing volleyball under the canopies of tall oak and spruce trees. I couldn't stop thinking about my boxcar-hopping fantasy. Really, I just wanted to take off and never return home to Warren Street. "If we coulda jumped into *one* boxcar, Carolyn, in September, we coulda told everyone goin' into fifth grade. Then they'd look up to us." Actually, I wanted to see Sister Rose again, my fifth-grade teacher at St. Joseph's school, and tell *her* all about my adventurous summer. Carolyn's shoulders were drooping, her head shaking in disappointment. I hated to see her feeling so badly 'cause of me. "It's all right."

"We can try again next week," she perked up.

"Sure! Maybe we can take snacks with us so we'll have more energy and you won't be so tired." I noticed the same lack of luster to her cheeks, still gray and sickly. "Let's get a drink!" Surely some water would bring back her color. My Grandma McCarten says that bending down and standing up always increases blood flow. After all, Carolyn's my best friend, and best friends have to do whatever they can for each other, right?

Stopping at a little hand-cranked water fountain, we gulped down velvety cold water to our gills. We splashed a few handfuls on our faces and throats, all the while swooshing away flies who woulda liked to drink the dryin' sweat on our arms and legs. All morning long, Carolyn and I had been hanging out around the Wild Side fishing hole in Henderson Park. Then we played T-ball and a game of baseball. Carolyn looked pooped. Maybe she had "too much exertion" as my Irish Grandpa McCarten always says With our stomachs growling and gurgling from hunger, we walked toward our homes down tree-lined Warren Street. The giant boughs stretched in bending ballerina beauty in the incoming storm and wind. Carolyn lived two houses from me, but the distance felt transcontinental as we tiptoed in front of Mad Lady's house across the street and stepped over huge cracks and upchucking tree roots. "Don't break your mother's back!" we joked.

We stopped at her house in front of her long inviting front porch and its white wooden swing and shiny chain. "Joyce, ya gonna come over tomorrow at three to watch Neil Armstrong walk on the moon?" She pointed high with longing eyes. We both had talked long and hard about what it would take for us to become astronauts. We made a pact. Whoever would reach outer space first would look down and wave *hi* at the other. Would that day ever happen? What would our futures look like? Would we *always* be friends?

"Sure I'll be over at your house at three!" I replied, picking up her dodge ball off the top step and bouncing it. We dashed to our usual spot in the driveway and began playing two square. As the ball slipped through her thin, dirt-smudged legs, I noticed my stepdad's Yellow taxicab burping slowly toward us. I dove into a row of bushes. "It's Peg-leg Al," I whispered as she jumped in behind me.

"Why's he home so early?" She set her hand on my shoulder and gained her balance.

"Probably to check on Mikey."

"What's wrong with *him?*"

I didn't want to talk about it, and I trembled and shrugged, recalling what happened this morning. Al had yelled at my brother Tommy in retaliation for what happened yesterday afternoon. A Volkswagen Beetle bumped our half-brother Mikey whose arm was now in a cast. Tommy was supposed to have been watching Mikey, but I guess Tommy got distracted or thought Mikey was on the lawn and not in the street. Ever since that time, Al had been in a fuming mood. This morning was the lid popping off the kettle for Peg-leg Al. With his bush-black forking eyebrows, he began screaming at Crazy Mary and Tommy. "Run, Tommy!" I shouted. Al chased him out of the house. When terrified Tommy turned a corner, Al, running weird because of his wooden leg, trapped him, caught him, lifted him high, and then threw him on the driveway. Crying, Tommy limped back into the house through Grandma McCarten's front entryway. Tommy got a rotten deal! After all, how can a nine-year-old kid watch a four-year-old kid hours on end when he himself is just a playin' kid?

"Rotten deal!" I fumed, sticking up my middle finger at ol' Peg-leg Al who'd lost half his leg in the Korean War. As his Yellow cab passed us, I saw his dark torso straighten in the driver's seat. But no—*no way* could he have seen me give him the finger! Another gust of storm-cool wind blew into our faces, and I wondered: *Would Tommy and I ever get outta this place?* I'd prayed that *many* times, waiting for God's answer.

"Joyce?" Carolyn's sea green eyes widened and her dirt-dried brown bangs jerked. "I hope ol' Al didn't see ya do that."

I waved off her concern. After all, I'd grown pretty tough through the years. "We're so far back. No way—"

"Joycie!" My mom's banshee cry made us look west toward busy Calumet Avenue.

"It's my mom." Crazy Mary had a high-pitch voice, the meanness in her. My belly turned to jelly.

"Joycie! Get over 'ere right now!" Her voice shrieked down the entire Warren Street.

A dizzy sickness welled up my throat. "Uh-oh, I better go."

Carolyn grabbed her ball, clutching it against her flat chest. Again, I noticed her pale cheeks, but I didn't think anything of it since we both had been running around in the dirt, and this past week, swimming at the Y six blocks down Hohman Avenue and a short jot down Cherry Street. *Swimming! That sounds fun!* "You got fifty cents to go swimming later?" I was thinking about the two boys we met there two days ago and the fun we had playing Marco Polo and doing wacky stunts off the diving board.

"I think so," she shrugged, picking a mint leaf off a bush by her front stairs and biting it. She had a way of twisting a bit when she was contemplating, as grandma McCarten would say whenever she saw someone just thinking.

"Joycie! *Now!*" My Mom's voice hit a crescendo.

"You better go," Carolyn sulked. Neither one of us had to say much about Crazy Mary. Carolyn knew. She glanced at the small brown bruise on my cheekbone, days old, but still smarting me.

Walking slowly down her driveway to the sidewalk, I felt like turning to the left and heading right back to the inviting railroad tracks. But I couldn't, and I hated bein' a chicken 'cause my dad wasn't any savior. And the only way outta Monster House, what I called home, the noisiest and most rambunctious house on the block, was to leave Warren Street for good. That was my prayer, once an hour, just like the monks and nuns used to sing psalms in medieval times. "I'll get some money and come back after supper," I shouted. We knew that time to be six o'clock. The YMCA had evening swim from six to eight.

Before my mom could blurt out another street-thundering name call, I stopped her. "Here I am. Is something wrong?" I swallowed hard. I saw her black, neck-length curly hair and a mean grimace on her pale-pure face. She *definitely* looked different, cocked at bit sideways, and standing in front of the white basement door. She had *something* behind her back. "Hi, Mom," I shook, saliva drying on my tongue, while I stayed a safe distance from her. She had angry wide eyes, always black, no color to her irises. I quickly remembered the story of the Irish Sealy her mom, my grandma Anne McCarten, once told me. Legend says there's a black, skin-smooth, magical Irish seal that since ancient times has been swimming along the shores of Galway Bay. Every fifty years, she seeks a mate to breed with so as to keep her kind from goin' extinct. When she spots a man who lights her fancy, she swims to him and allows the poor unsuspecting soul to pet her and snuggle up to her. Once touched, the Sealy turns into an alluring, beautiful seaweed-clad woman. Of course, under her spell, the man falls hopelessly in love with her. But no matter whom she marries and the number of beautiful dark-skinned children she has, the Sealy is always unhappy. She's suspended between the allure of the sea and the stability of rock-solid ground. The sea is her wild nature and calling; this earthly life the trappings of reality with no escape. Life is never the same with a crazed dark-haired Sealy who's always divided between Earth and supernatural places. That's Crazy Mary, my mom.

Mom suddenly unleashed a shotgun from behind her back.

I gasped. My intestines churned to the contortions of a down-spiraling carnival ride.

She pointed the gun at my face and cocked it—*clutch-crunch*—ready to shoot. "Don't you dare, you f=#%&!* b#@%!*, *ever* stick a finger up at my husband again!"

I felt melted, somewhere onto the cracked driveway—my body emptying into a shell. I'd never be the same for *anyone* and to *anyone* again. Where I found the next words, an angel musta infused 'em into me to calm her down and reel her back to sanity. "Sorry, Mom. *Please*, Mom!"

Dazed, Crazy Mary released the shotgun's bullet and the gun dropped to her side. She opened the weather-stained basement door, and, like the hunchback of Notre Dame, probably aware that the next-door neighbor might be watching, dashed into the basement.

I couldn't stop shaking and peed my pants. Rain began to fall in chilly drizzles that changed into pounding drops on my face, arms, and legs—the Heavenly waters cool compresses that brought my skin back to tingling reality. *What do I do now? Go inside? Go to Carolyn's?* That thought triggered what I'd told Carolyn earlier. I needed to find fifty cents so I could go swimming tonight. After all, two boys had been there last night and we were hoping would be there tonight. *Gee, I wonder what's happening to me. Last year, we made fun of boys. Now, we want to see 'em?* Sneaking up the front porch and passing cigar-smokin' grandpa McCarten who was sitting in his glider swing and listening to a White Sox game, I crept up the grand oak staircase, sidled into Mom's bedroom, opened her black-varnished dresser drawer and grabbed two-quarters out of her small crystal coin jar. Quickly I changed my shorts. All the while, I cringed as I listened to all the yellin' and screamin' goin' on between my mom and Peg-leg Al arguing over what to have for supper. I quickly dashed down the stairs, but I knew full well that I'd have to return at some point before supper to tell her where I was going or else she'd have the broom to my head. Running to Carolyn's basement door, I knocked like a lunatic.

"Whatchya doin' here so early?" She whispered, looking dark under the eyes. "I've been working on something for you and me, but it's not ready yet," she grinned.

I felt my shoulders pinch like the time I had to climb the gym rope to the ceiling. "My Mom went bonkers on me again, the witch." I kicked the bottom stair as we jumped to the basement floor. When I stood up with the wooden-slatted rafter section looming above us, I saw ten lit candles around two seat cushions and a tiny footstool in the center of the dark room. On it burned a small tea candle with a pin cushion on the left. "What's goin' on?"

Through spooky-wide energetic eyes, she waved for me to sit down opposite her. The basement had a dank smell—detergent and dust and mildew. The candlelight gleamed and glowed with ghost-story quality. Carolyn *definitely* had an amazing event she'd been planning for us for quite some time. "Ya wanna become blood sisters?"

The pincushion and needles on the stepstool enlarged in my sight, reminding me of shot time at the doc's office. I recalled an Indian ceremony I'd seen on TV, wherein a Sioux chief bonded himself in blood with a white man; but they didn't use pins, only a long-blade knife. Compared to that show, a little stick shouldn't hurt, right? "Okay. Let's do it," I replied, sticking my pointer finger at her.

Quickly, she pulled a pin out of the red cushion. Setting the long needle inside the yellow part of the tea-candle to sterilize it...and with shaking fingers...she slowly pulled out the pin. She stuck herself, and out oozed a tiny drop of blood. "Ye-ouch," she said, shoving the blood-dripping mess in front of me.

I acted fast. After following her example, I set my finger next to hers. "Now what?"

"We put 'em together," she smiled.

"What'll that do?" I stuck my dark red finger onto her bleeding finger.

"It means," she began through serious sea-green eyes, "that no matter where we go, or what we do, or whatever we become…we'll *always* be together. We're blood sisters."

"Blood sisters!" I repeated. Watching our blood mingle and drop, I suddenly felt a weird sense of belonging. Heaven knows, I *never* felt this kinda connection with my mom *or* dad. Wow! Special! *Finally*, I had a best friend for life…forever.

"Yep," she said blinking, her eyes tearing.

We separated our sticky fingers. I didn't know whether her blood and my blood could pass through the skin barrier to change whatever had made us into who God created us to be. I'd have to ask Mr. Tobias that question when I'd enter sixth grade next month.

"Carolyn!" Her mother called.

Carolyn shot up like a flying fish. "Gotta Go. Super." She wiped her finger on her shorts and a little bloodstain appeared.

"You better wash that off right now with soap and water," I began, "or else your mom'll *really* be mad. My grandma said that blood's like peach juice. It don't come out if you don't wash it out right away."

Carolyn's mom appeared on the basement landing, and Carolyn and I squashed all the candle lights. "Is that you, Joycie?"

I could see her flushed face and quizzical body language. She was obviously puzzled as to what we were doing and straining to see us. Also, her left eye had a left-slanted disorder of some sort. I never knew whether she was looking at me or at another place beyond me, making me feel on edge. "Yes, Mrs. Clark, but I'm headin' home. It's super time at my house, too. But I'll be back in an hour, 'cause

Carolyn and I are goin' swimming at the Y." I didn't have to ask her for permission. We'd been swimming almost every night for the last month, so I already knew she'd let Carolyn go.

As I walked up the back stairs to the entrance to my house, I heard moaning. I stopped to try and figure out whether it was safe to take another step, or like usual, drop back like a Vietnam soldier knowing his end might be at hand. Through the sorrowful moans and groans, I breathed the ion-scented stormy air, humid, but also predicting fall days to come. The rain had stopped, but clouds were teardrops on the horizon with the Sun's light skipping heartbeats of golden rays through the late afternoon. Hopping the last steps onto the wooden landing, I spotted the scuffed white door, wide open, and mom sitting bent over in a chair. She had her hands over her face and was deep in the throngs of hot crying. Looking past her, I couldn't believe my eyes! Someone had tipped over the *entire* oak table. Mom had cooked fried chicken, green beans, and boiled corn…now all a mishmash on the black and white checkered floor— glass stew. No one could eat that, and I was hungry. What to do? No one was in sight, not even Grandma McCarten from downstairs, Al, or any of my brothers and sisters. Where'd everyone go?

"What happened, Mom?" I asked softly swallowing hard, keeping my distance. *That shotgun could be anywhere!*

She peeked at me through her arthritic fingers. "Oh, Al got upset again."

I tiptoed gently over the white mess of glass stew and dishes. All I really cared about was getting my swimsuit and a towel. Then, I could run down the center staircase, leave, and not come back until after ten. No one would care, and this would all be over, as usual. "Sorry about all this, Mom. I'm goin' swimming with Carolyn." As she wailed some more, I dashed into my room—the room I share with two brothers—grabbed my suit and ran downstairs to grandma and grandpa's place. Smelling the scents of corned beef and cabbage, I stopped when my mouth salivated like a starving dog.

"Is that you, Joycie?" Grandma called in her Irish accent.

Grandpa was quiet as usual and reclining in the living room. He was smoking his pipe and watching the black and white newscast of the astronauts who were in deep space and approaching the moon. I grew so excited. *Tomorrow is the big day!*

"Yeah, Grandma, it's me!" I spotted leftovers smothered in ketchup. Hey, who cares who'd been eating 'em and what cooties were rollin' round. I was deathly hungry. I stuffed my mouth full, chewing until my chipmunk cheeks felt like they'd pop, and crammed the rest of the luscious red meat, orange-sweet carrots, and deep green cabbage into two napkins. I'd finish it all off at Carolyn's place. "I'm goin' to the Y, Grandma. Bye!"

"When ya comin' back, Joycie?" She peeked at me from the kitchen. She was thin like a broomstick, had crooked teeth, wore her gray hair in a net, and had the deepest blue eyes I'd ever seen. How did Sealy Mary ever come from Grandma's pure stock, I'd never know.

"The usual time," I said, hiding the stolen food under my towel.

Sneering at me as if I'd stolen diamonds and shaking her forefinger, she squinted hard. "You're a mischievous one, Joycie. I know you're up to something."

"I'm up to nothin', Grandma, *really*." I slowly backed away toward the stained-glass front door. Through more of her cautious talk about what I was going to become if I kept up with my mischievous ways, I said a quick goodbye and then dashed out the church-thick door. As my mom's upstairs wailing trickled to nothingness, I ran to Carolyn's place, all the while pecking at those delicious leftovers in my napkin, their sleepy effects digesting in my belly making me drowsy. I had to fight their spellbinding effects. Carolyn and I had plans! We were both looking so forward to playing water games at the Y.

She beat me to the door and jumped down her front steps. She reminded me a bit of young version of Sally Field in *The Flying Nun*. "Let's get outta here!"

As we jogged down the street with our towels rolled under our arms and I ate the rest of my stolen dinner, I couldn't help but know for certain that something just wasn't right with Carolyn. Even after dinner, she looked pale. This time, I was going to talk about it. "Why are you so sickly looking? Is something wrong?"

She waved off my concern. Running made blood flow a bit into her cheeks, draining the paste gray from her face. "I probably just got a bit o' the flu my mom says. She really didn't want me swimming tonight, but I told her I'd do the dishes tomorrow night and stay home."

"Ahh," I moaned. "Well, at least we'll have a blast tonight!" We ran across busy Hohman Avenue and began our usual shortcut through five yards and three alleys toward the Y. In the southwest, the Sun rounded over the trees. The hot rays had melted those threatening thunderclouds into a steady haze on the horizon, and God rays filtered down to us, along with half a rainbow in the sky. I'd never seen such a sky-high drizzle of a prism, and we paused in awe. As the rainbow dissipated, I felt the effects of the blood-sister bond we'd cemented earlier and my eyes stung with tears. I had a crazy mom, an absent dad, a mean peg leg Al, and weasels for brothers and sisters. The only *real* close person was Carolyn.

"Yep, we're best friends forever," she said, an energetic gleam firing in her sea-green eyes. "Come on! I'll race ya to the Y!" She moved with extra momentum as if she had to prove she was completely fine.

Still, I overtook her. As we rounded the corner to the Y, I could see a long line at the door, and the two boys we'd seen yesterday standing at the end of the line. Stopping and gaining our breath, I whispered to her as we approached them, "I think they're waiting for us."

She giggled. "Looks like it."

She had a nervous quiver in her voice, and my stomach felt queasy. I even got a little numb in the arms! Weird. I told her that, and then, as we neared the two boys who looked all dressed up and polished like on Sundays, she whispered, "I feel the same way."

I stomped a little. "I don't get it, Carolyn, but I think it's cause we like 'em. It's not like you and me being friends, though. There's something different goin' on here." I felt a bit angry that I couldn't stop the excitement, and I guess the downright powerlessness I felt just by looking at Michael Landon. I recalled an expression I once heard a TV star say, *weak in the knees.*

"I heard, that feeling weak and sick happens when girls like boys." Appearing to be under the spell of James Nichols who was standing soldier-like next to Michael Landon, Carolyn had big round eyes on "Jimmy" who'd just graduated from sixth grade.

"I don't *like* feeling weak and sick, though," I said, my jaw tensing and hands tightening. "If I want that happening to me, I'd just turn around and go back home. Besides, yesterday, I didn't feel this way about Michael." Both boys were now yards away. "Not at all."

She coughed two times and trembled as a great commotion stirred through the line. The doors opened for the evening swim, and people began paying the attendant.

When I approached Michael, I noticed a warm charm to him. *He wasn't this way yesterday!* "Hey Joyce," he smiled through dark eyes and round sunburnt cheeks.

I had watched him play baseball over the years, never believing we'd *ever* be so uncomfortable with each other. "Hi, Michael, how's it going?" He didn't answer at first, and a questioning expression shone in his eyes. There, in a long zig-zagging line, with so many people chattering about superficial things, Michael and I seemed to melt into a thick uneasiness like being in a funeral procession but not wanting to leave. He answered me, but I couldn't hear one word through all my stomach upset and nervous mind chatter. I just kept nodding and toe-tapping the sidewalk. Then, we arrived at the girl behind the iron gate. "I've got this," he said, paying for me proudly. I noticed Jimmy paying for Carolyn, too. She had a coy Gidget smile with a Barbie shyness playing all over her. Wow, must she like Jimmy in the same way I was beginning to fancy Michael Landon. Obviously, none of us knew what to do about our new feelings and what to say next. One thing for sure, I *didn't* understand *why* Michael was paying *my* way into the Y. But before I asked him, several thoughts stopped me: maybe he's just being nice; maybe he likes me and is paying for me like Bud Anderson pays for his dates on *Father Knows Best*; or, maybe I should just accept his gift and sneak my mom's quarters back into her dresser so I don't get smacked.

"Thanks, Michael," I said, and we walked into separate bathrooms to change.

After several fun diving board competitions, we all began the slow walk home. Michael and Jimmy insisted on "escorting us home."

Through small talk, with Carolyn and Jimmy walking yards behind Michael and me, we turned down Warren Street. "Do you have Mr. Tobias's class in September?" Michael asked. "He's good. He teaches all the subjects, but I really liked him as a religion teacher. You know, he studied to be a priest at one time. *I'm* thinking about being a priest."

"Oh yeah? Hm." Those words made me think extra hard about Michael being my boyfriend. Priests lead different lives than regular men. What was he doin' with me if he was considering being one of them? I remembered what Carolyn told me earlier. During one of our Marco Polo games, she said, "Jimmy just asked me to be his girlfriend!" She giggled like it was Christmas.

"What did *you* say?" I glanced at blushing Michael, smiling at me. Every expression indicated he was planning to ask *me* to be *his* girlfriend. *Gosh, all this girlfriend-boyfriend stuff is so confusing and complicated. Is this kind of chaos always going to exist between boys and* me?

"I said yes," her nose perked. I think she learned all her shy and coy expressions from TV. Where else? I sure didn't see her mom and dad swooning over each other that way. "I think Michael is going to ask you to be his girlfriend sometime tonight."

I folded my arms. "Under *no* circumstance will I let Michael Landon even *touch* my hand!"

"Yeah, right," she said.

As I finished remembering that conversation, Michael told me more about his ideas of joining the priesthood. Out of the blue, he grabbed my hand tightly. "Ouch!" I said, breaking out of his sweaty grip.

"Sorry," he said softly. I could barely see his eyes. The streetlights were flooding the treetops but not lighting the sidewalks.

I felt woozy, like butterflies fluttering in my stomach, and my arms tingled. We stopped walking, he pulled me close to him, and he kissed me on the lips. I thought a wet frog had smacked me! Just then, I glanced at Carolyn, kissing Jimmy with her arms around his neck. Then, I kissed Michael Landon right back!

"Wow," he exclaimed, his surfer-thin body reeling. Time stopped, and my heart beat lifted to my throat. The world was spinning, and I never wanted off.

"Joycie!" This time, Mom's voice rang out clear as a bell because of the light traffic on Calumet Avenue.

I cringed at the sound of my mother's harpy voice. "That's my mom." Quickly, I wiped off my lips and stepped onto the sidewalk out of the shadows of two tall oak trees. Forever, I'd *always* remember the spot of my first kiss. "I better go," I stammered. Dreamy-eyed and star-struck, Carolyn slowly parted from Jimmy's arms, and the two boys joined forces to begin their walk home. In the funnel vision of a white streetlight, a pale ghostly appearance fell over Carolyn's face. Was this odd skin color the same as earlier in the day? *Naw, it couldn't be. She's fine. She swam the entire night. She's fine.*

"Joycie!" My mom was right in front of Carolyn's house.

"I better go, Carolyn."

"See ya tomorrow, Joyce," she said, twirling like a happy Cinderella.

"I'll be over after breakfast." I sprinted to my towering dark mother.

Looking back, I saw Carolyn wave bye and dash up her stairs. I almost ran into my mother who was leering at me under a funnel of streetlight. "What are you doing?" She obviously had seen the boys leave.

"Nothing," I bowed, kicking a bulge in the sideway.

I smelled alcohol on her breath. She always drank at nights. Who wouldn't with Al, all those screamin' kids, and her misery. "You know, Joycie, you can get pregnant kissing a boy."

Pregnant? I recalled her rotund stomach that looked she'd eaten a reindeer. I never wanted that! So, I decided, I'd never be kissin' Michael Landon *ever* again! But, how was I ever going to stop that? I *hated* the way he made me feel, and I really *liked* the way he made me feel. I guess this is just the way it is between girls and boys, and always will be.

An hour after being in the house and watching TV, I saw cycling red and white lights down the street. "I think all the commotion is coming from Carolyn's house," my mom said, peering out the second-story window.

I didn't even look but sprinted down the back stairs and two houses over to where paramedics were wheeling a white-draped body into the ambulance. "What happened?!" I screamed, running toward Carolyn's parents who rushing to their car.

Her mom was madly crying, her father shaking as if he'd been fighting a vampire. "She just collapsed!" her mom cried through the whirling ambulance lights. "I'll call you tomorrow, Joycie and let you know what's happening."

I began crying my eyes out, *balling*, as my dad calls it. "Is she, okay?" I believed I would drop down dead if anything would happen to Carolyn Clark.

"I think we got to her *just* in time," Carolyn's thin dad said, starting the car. "We'll keep ya posted, Joycie."

"First thing in the morning!" her mother added.

"I'll be at the hospital at first light!" I shouted, their car's rear wheels bouncing over the driveway hump. The ambulance and their car turned north on Calumet Avenue toward St. Margaret's hospital less a mile away. I couldn't sleep all night. I kept thinking: *Was there something I coulda done throughout the day to have stopped this*? I stared at the street light on Calumet Avenue, listened to cricket calls, and tried repeating the rattling of the locusts reviving out of their hibernation states. Suddenly, I realized, I couldn't have done a thing to help Carolyn. I didn't know something serious was wrong with her! When I'd asked her about everything abnormal I'd observed, she said she had the flu, or wasn't eating right, or didn't get enough sleep. Shoot…all those things happen to everyone at some time, right? Doesn't mean an ambulance is gonna show up, right?

The next morning, I rode my bike to St. Margaret's. Next door was St. Joseph's, my school. I said a prayer while riding the elevator up to the floor where the candy striper told me to go. "God, I've never asked you for anything except to make my Dad take me and Tom away from Crazy Mary so we can live with him. But now, I'd give up that prayer if you'd heal Carolyn. Amen."

Sneaking around two nurses' stations, finding her room, and stepping inside, I saw Carolyn hooked up to *two* monitors! The *beep beep*s of her heart nearly made me faint!

"Joyce, what are ya doin' here?" her mother asked. She was worn, her dress wrinkled cotton.

"Carolyn's my best friend," I said, shaking, fearful she'd throw me out of the sterile-smelling room. "I just had to make sure she's still alive." I broke down, crying.

Carolyn's dad walked up and put his arm gently around my shoulders. "It'll be all right, Joycie. I know Carolyn will be just fine."

I had a dad, but he'd never been around much for me, and he sure as heck didn't have a consoling bone in his body, just huffy dreariness, and stiffness. In that minute, Carolyn's dad became *my* dad. "See? She's breathin' and just fine." He patted my arm. "She's diabetic. We never realized it. She's sick now—"

"But with medications," her mom interrupted, "Carolyn's gonna be fine."

"She'll probably be home tomorrow or the next day!" her father added cheerfully. "She just needs rest now."

I dashed to Carolyn's bedside and touched her hand. She had a rosy color in her cheeks, making her angelic. "Carolyn," I bent down whispering, "I'm lighting a candle for ya at church today. Just get well, and get home soon, 'cause life without ya will be just *plain* boring. Besides, we gotta plan another time to hop a boxcar." I think she heard me, 'cause I saw a little grin. Or maybe, that lip lift was just gas, as my grandma would say kids often pass in their sleep. "Hurry up and get well. We're blood sisters. Like ya said, forever. You just *can't* leave for Heaven yet!" Her parents assured me again that she'd be fine. Strange, though, how I have difficulty taking people at their word.

I rode my bike slowly home. The traffic on Calumet Avenue was never ending horn honking and weird men whistling. The next morning, bright and early, outta the blue, my dad George and his girlfriend Cecilia showed up for a surprise visitation. As a newscaster announces a fast-approaching category-5 tornado, Tom and I leaped into his Chevy convertible. Then, "Ceil" as my dad, Georgie Porgie, called her, noticed how thin, bruised, and malnourished we were. On the twenty-five minute drive to my Grandma and Grandpa's farmhouse in Hannah—my sanctuary—she said after a prolonged silent period, "George, you *can't* let these kids go back there." She had warm brown eyes with a cozy expression on her face. They began to whisper so Tommy and I couldn't hear them.

I kept repeating in my mind: *Security and protection at last! Really though?* I kept pinching myself out of the dream!

"We'll figure out where they can stay until we get married in a few days," she said.

Wow, so fast…getting married? Considering I could barely kiss Michael Landon and wanted to run from him like a frightened mouse, how could Georgie Porgie make such a hasty decision when he'd just met "Her Majesty?" That's what I nicknamed her two weeks ago because he always opened *every* door for her and seated her for lunch and dinner. *This is wife number three. Should I tell Georgie that he's got serious problems!* Later on, after God granted me my prayer, I learned some cold hard facts about life. Whatever Ceil wanted, Her Majesty got.

Now, back to that day when Tom and I left Warren Street like a twister might level that house. Ceil instructed us to pack up as much as we could and to tell our mom the following: "Grandma and Grandpa said we could stay a week with them on their farm for the last vacation before school starts. Please let us go! Besides, it'll give you a little vacation from us so you can rest up." We packed our roller skates and ice skates. I shoved my clothes up my blouse so I appeared triple-D sized, and Tom crammed his clothes down his pants until he appeared twenty pounds heavier than before and muscle man strong.

The first day away from Warren Street, peace and calmness flowed over me as if Jesus and His angels were hovering. I felt so happy! Until I remembered Carolyn in the hospital and *our* plans to watch the moon landing. I had seen the lunar landing earlier with my aunts. I called her, but she'd been discharged.

I dialed her house phone. "Carolyn! Are you okay?" I felt frantic 'cause I couldn't go back to Crazy Mary's. For sure she'd realize what had happened, lock me up, and probably never let me see my dad again.

Carolyn's voice sounded strong. "Yeah, I'm fine. Hey, when ya comin' back? I called your mom to see if ya wanted to come over and watch the moon landing yesterday, but she said you went to your grandparent's house with your dad."

I could picture her face—so surfer tanned and her body strong from her new treatments. I couldn't muster up the courage to tell her, "Never, I hope." I changed the subject. "What happened to you?" I clenched the phone. "Did your blood make too much sugar?"

"Sorta," she replied. "I have to take medicine in shots once a day from now on."

"Once a day?" I grimaced. "Ya mean, with a needle? That kinda shot?"

"Yep."

"Drats," I moaned, and then I told her about the remarkable miracle God performed to sweep me permanently away from Monster house. "We'll be staying with our Aunt Liz until Georgie and Her Majesty get married."

After a shockingly happy screech, her voice turned quiet, probably fearful of her mom overhearing her. "Can you ask your dad to drive you over tomorrow? Please? I can't go swimming for a few weeks the doctor said, but we *can* do something else like play cards. Your mom doesn't even have to know you're here!" I could imagine her round face full of pleading. She was missing me already. I was missing her, too.

"He can't," I huffed. "He's at the steel mill. That's where he met Her Majesty." Then, fear leaped into my chest.

"What's wrong?" Carolyn asked.

I began to think terrifying thoughts. "In a week, Crazy Mary will learn we aren't coming back and throw a block-long temper fit."

"Oh for sure!" Carolyn said.

I realized, though, that she wouldn't miss us. She'd just miss her support money and punching bags. I gasped. "Uh-oh, you know what?"

"What?"

"She'll probably show up at *your* place to interrogate ya, like spies

148

extracting information on *Mission Impossible*," I said. "Crazy Mary'll push *hard* to get you to make you tell her we're at my Aunt Liz's house. My dad doesn't want her to know where we're at until he sees a lawyer, he said." I believed I'd just swallowed a raw egg! "So, don't tell 'er," I choked. "Please, don't!"

She took several long laborious breaths. "Of course I won't. I promise! After all, we're blood sisters. And we'll always *be* blood sisters, no matter if we *never* see each other again." After a few more minutes of exchanging encouraging words, we hung up.

In the weeks thereafter, Carolyn and I talked, but not as frequently as when I lived two houses down from her. Six months later, after I started Wilbur Wright Junior High in Munster, I called Carolyn. A horrible tune resounded, followed by an automatic recording. "The number you have dialed has been disconnected. Please check with the operator for further information."

I never heard from Carolyn again. Twenty-five years later, I did, however, get up the nerve to ask my half-brother Mikey if he had ever discovered what happened to Carolyn Clark.

"I heard she got married and lives in northeastern Indiana," he answered.

That answer didn't help me. Even today, she's invisible on social media.

North, south, east, west...wherever Carolyn Clark—or whatever her name is now—lives, we remain blood sisters. One day, I'll meet her in the afterlife. We'll relive our fun-filled days on Warren Street— the happy times. Isn't that what everyone wants? To see the people we once knew but could never find, and who've been lost to time...in Heaven?

# # #

J.P. Osterman was one of five finalists for the Patrick D. Smith Literary Award. She won a Rupert Hughes Award for *The Matter Stream*, now the Nelta Series: *First Communication. Battlefield Matrix*, and *Astrocity Sagan.* Her one-act play, *The Man Next to Me,* won First Place at the Southern California Writers' Conference, now also *Pete's Crossroad.* Including *God Designed*, J.P. has written ten novels, one exploring Mars in *Cosmic Rift.* She released two short-story books, *Commuter Collection* and *Pareidolia.* Her novels include *The Screaming Stone* and *Corporate Revenge.* More information about J.P. is available online at www.jposterman.com.

A TALE OF THREE BARBARAS

By Emily Pippin

It seems that there are times in our life when we know several people with the same name. Thinking about good friends, I found that there was a Barbara in each stage of my life who was without a doubt my best friend. What made each of them a friend? It was not what they could do for me but because of who they were and what we shared. A friend right there beside me doing the special things with me. And as I thought about it, I said, *That's what a friend is, someone "being with" and "doing things together."* And memories flooded my thoughts about everything we meant to each other.

My family moved from Vienna, Virginia, to Washington, D.C., at the start of my junior year in high school. I had been well established at Fairfax High School, active in clubs, participant and often winner in talent shows, with lots of friends from my "class" of society. Now I was thrust into Calvin Coolidge High School, a huge school with many students from higher socioeconomic families. It was a lonely few weeks. The one class that I thought I might like was advanced creative writing and speech, what would now be considered an AP course. And I did enjoy it. PE frightened me—archery, field hockey, bowling, swimming, and square dancing! I couldn't do any of those things and I dreaded that class every day. However, Miss Snodgrass (yes, that was her name) was an encourager, and I did become a reasonably good archer.

When we were assigned a partner to learn to square dance, I went home and said, "Mom I want to drop out of school." Of course it fell on deaf ears! I was paired up with Barbara Penney, outgoing, tall, with straight clipped hair, and a very good dancer. Everything I was not! As I struggled to learn the dance steps, Barbara patiently kept telling me to "just relax and you will enjoy it." Her words were prophetic. Slowly I relaxed and became sure of myself and began to enjoy learning the square dance calls. Suddenly I found myself in an eight-person square that had been named the best in the class. It was a thrill. But the next blow came when we were told that our square had been chosen to go to the junior high schools in the D.C. area to demonstrate square dancing. Well. I knew what "Duck for the oyster, Dive for the clam" was and that is just what I wanted to do–duck! Barbara wouldn't let me back out. We became a great square-dancing pair that year and great friends.

One day I was telling Barbara that my sister and I loved to sing and harmonize. "I dance with the D.C. Recreation Association at all the military bases. Why don't you and your sister audition? They will love you." She hadn't heard us sing together but she had heard me sing solos in the talent shows and her enthusiasm was all that I needed. We auditioned with Amourette Miller who was in charge of the singers and the rest is history.

For the next three years we sang at Fort Belvoir, Fort Myer, Fort Meade, Walter Reed, Quantico, and Andrews Air Force Base. The performers and our coaches met at the lobby of the Washington Hotel on 15th Street between F Street and Pennsylvania Avenue, and there we were picked up by a driver with a motor pool bus from the base we would be performing at and taken to the performance location. Some of the buses were good. Others left a lot to be desired. Sometimes the bus broke down, and after one winter show, we waited by the side of the road till another bus came from the motor pool to get us. It was 3:00 a.m. when we finally reached the hotel. Barbara was always in the dance team. Our friendship continued to grow closer as we rode the bumpy camp buses during those years. You might say we were inseparable. And she kept being the encourager. The camp shows increased from Friday and Saturday to include sometimes Tuesday, Thursday and occasionally a Sunday evening.

We spent time together at each other's houses after school and on weekends when we weren't in the shows. We went with our youth group on beach outings. We even started buying matching shirts!

When I enrolled in The King's College in Delaware, the team had a farewell party for me after the final show, including gifts and a cake that said "So Long to the Singing Scholar." That was the only time that I remember when our coaches allowed us to intermingle with the servicemen after the shows. Our goodbye was very sad. Barbara and I had become fast friends.

Barbara continued her dancing, became a veterinarian, and remained in Maryland. Last year I called her and memories came flooding back as we reminisced about those bus trips, sometimes uneventful, and sometimes cold, stranded, hungry, and in need of roadside help. She will always fill the "Friend" spot from my high school days.

Now college alum, I was married, we had moved to Newton, Massachusetts, and we had a precious little daughter who loved the ventriloquist, Shari Lewis and her lamb. And into my life came my second Barbara–Barbara Lamb! She was from Maine and had a dry sense of humor that was made even more humorous by her Maine accent. Barbara was a lamb not in name only but also in kindness, love, gentleness, and playfulness. She became our baby sitter for the next four years, and we all grew to love her. She cared for our children–now three of them–and we were never at a loss for something to do.

Baby number four came along at the same time that the other half of our duplex was rented to a family with unruly children. After one of them put my son in a cardboard box and began stabbing through the box with the kitchen knife, I said, "This is enough. We have to move." We moved into a very large ten-room house and there was a little "apartment" on the first floor that had probably been the maid's quarters. Barbara moved in with us and she became BaBa, my young children's live-in baby sitter and like a second mommy.

My husband worked two jobs, so Barbara and I would play games in the evening after the children were in bed. Our favorite was taking a long word out of the newspaper and seeing who could make the most words out of its letters in five minutes. We could play that for hours. I didn't drive so on shopping day every week I would walk the mile to the grocery, time it just right so that I could have my shopping done and be at the store entrance when Barbara arrived. She would use her lunch hour to pick me up, drive home, help carry in the groceries and then go back to work!

An angel of mercy she was to me then besides a good friend. We planned parties together, went on picnics together, attended activities at the church and the children's school together, and even made costumes for my husband's plays together. Barbara had taken a permanent place in our family and it seemed she would be with our family forever. And what a joy that was.

My husband accepted a teaching position in Fort Wayne, Indiana. Many tears were shed when we said goodbye to our dear Barbara who would become my lifelong friend. And the tears continued to be shed after we had moved to Fort Wayne as our two-year old wondered why "my BaBa doesn't come home from work every day."

So we planned a three-week summer camping trip the following summer, and you guessed it. Barbara joined us as we traveled through Wisconsin, Minnesota, South Dakota, and Wyoming. Seven people in a Buick station wagon with two tents and all the equipment tied on the top. And we never stayed in one campground more than three days! It was great fun; our now three-year-old Brett was happy that his BaBa was once again with us; and my husband was thankful to have another driver. Me? I was filled with joy having my dear friend with us. And I was again reminded that she was the embodiment of I Peter 3:4, "the unfading beauty of a gentle and quiet spirit, which is of great worth in God's sight."

That year a new Christian school opened, and we enrolled our children into second, fourth and seventh grades. The following year the principal asked, "Would you be willing to quit your job at the Salvation Army Citadel and begin teaching for us?" *Would I!* Music was my love and teaching was my dream. That would mean vacations and summers off when the children were home so I could spend it doing things with them. I joyfully began teaching.

The school continued to grow and needed additional space for classes, so, after three years, we had to move from the church on the north side of town where we had been meeting to two places on the south side of town. That meant I had to travel to two separate locations–and I didn't drive. How would I get from one place to the other?

That fall I went in to the opening faculty meetings with much apprehension. The administrator introduced each of us and we began to get acquainted. Enter my third Barbara. The next four days we all met, planned, decorated rooms, looked over curriculum and learned about the new teachers. Now this young vivacious teacher who would be teaching Spanish was uniquely different from the rest of us. I wasn't quite sure about her. She was dressed in the style of the 70s– black designer stockings, sweater blouse that came down to the hips, a long belt that was more an accent of the waist to hip look than serving any purpose, a shoulder purse with a gold metal chain for the strap, and long streaked blond hair that hung all around her face. She had an infectious laugh that seemed to go along with her style. She was fascinating.

I was told that she would be teaching Spanish at the second campus during the same time periods as I would be teaching music so we would be riding back and forth together every day. She was not part of my "Christian" culture and I wasn't sure I wanted to ride with her every day. I want to teach but it seemed it was going to have its problems!

This is perhaps the time when I have been more wrong about someone that any other time in my life. She became my dearest friend. Barbara was and still is a lovely person, beautiful on the inside as well as the outside, caring, and never lacking a smile, a laugh, or an encouraging word. Riding in the van to our classes one day, I asked, "Barbara, you are so unconventional and individualistic, with such determined opinions and ideas, how did you last even one week at Bob Jones University?" Her answer changed the way I look at life. "Well, I chose to go to that school. No one forced me to go. So when I went, I knew that part of going there meant obeying the rules. So I did just that."

If we could all just look at life with that attitude. The world doesn't owe us anything. We make choices and when we are willing to fit in, strive for our goals, and not feel "entitled," we will be happy. And we will be able to serve the Lord.

Barbara started dating a wonderful young man named Kenneth who did not live in Fort Wayne. When he came into town, he stayed at our home. Now our children had their own Barbie and Ken "dolls" in their lives. I recall the first night Ken slept on our living room sofa. The next morning I asked him how he slept.

"Not very well," he chuckled. "The clock woke me up every fifteen minutes."

I was horrified. I had forgotten to stop the grandfather clock that he had shared the living room with! From then on, the chimes of the clock were silenced every weekend for the next several months.

Our Barbie and Ken "dolls" were married the following year. I still get cards and letters from them at Christmas time. Every picture is one that is a surprise because they are often dressed in some unique fashion. And Barbara is still bubbling over with laughter in each one of the pictures. She is truly the living proof of Proverbs 17:22 that "A cheerful heart is good medicine."

The three Barbaras—my good friends—one a retired veterinarian living in Taneytown, Maryland, who shared so many high school activities including entertaining the military troops with me, one who lived in Maine, became my children's BaBa, married, had two children and has now gone to her reward in Heaven, and the Barbie doll who is still married to her Ken, has children, and grandchildren. Each time I think of her, I hear her love of life and her laughter, and I smile about how wrong first impressions can be.

I am glad that these 'special friends' have remained in my life regardless of how many years and miles separate us. Friends. That's what it's all about.

# # #

Emily Pippin, retired high school teacher, taught music, art, Bible, and directed choirs and musicals for 34 years. She holds a Bachelor of Arts in Music from The King's College in New York City, and a Masters in Music Education from St. Francis in Fort Wayne, Indiana. Besides her love of music, she enjoys family history and has written five genealogy books, devotionals for CBN, and numerous articles. She and her husband live in Palm Bay, FL.

FRIENDSHIP'S GLUE

By Leon Pippin

"Hey, Leon, wanna go fishing?"

It had been a long, cold, lonely few months since we moved from Missouri. We were in Nashville, Michigan, and everything was new. New town, new church, new school, new teachers, even new lighting that was electric, and new fears that grew with each different entry into my life.

Henry Cowell at Thornapple Lake c 1948

Besides my two brothers, Glenn and Dick, I had no friends, and I didn't know what to do in this town. So when Henry Cowell, a friend I met in school, asked me to go fishing, I jumped at the chance. We went fishing at Thornapple Lake that had great boats and some nice buildings surrounding it. And we started catching our quota of catfish, whitefish, and bass. I was once again doing things outdoors, and Michigan was feeling a little less threatening. We walked the railroad tracks and tried to see who could walk the rails longer without falling off. We walked through the cemetery on the way to Henry's house and sometimes we sat on one of the stones and talked about life. We almost mirrored David and Jonathan's relationship in the Bible. Henry became my first friend.

That fall, we started going pheasant hunting. Well, actually Henry did the hunting and I just went along for the excitement of watching him. He had a gun and was pretty good at hitting the desired target. I did not have a gun and probably couldn't have used it even if I did have one. But the thrill of tramping through the woods and watching for the pheasants as we came to a clearing was worth every moment. And when Henry shot a pheasant and it fell to the ground, it was pure excitement. Henry always took the pheasant home, cleaned it, and his mom fixed a pheasant dinner on Sunday! I can't remember if I ever tasted that pheasant or not, but Henry's mom was a good cook so I know it must have been delicious.

Winter snows fell and the Thornapple Lake froze over. Time for my friend and I to try two other outdoor activities: ice skating and sledding. Getting our skates laced up without being too loose or too tight was an interesting activity in itself. Finally ready, we stood up, and confidently began to "sail across the lake" on our skates. Well, some of the time we were skating with our ankles upright and our skates secure under our feet. Much of the time we fell and "sailed" across on our behinds! Laughter ensued as we got up and tried again. I had enjoyed the book Hans Brinker and the Silver Skates that my fourth grade teacher had read to the class when I lived in Missouri. So I shared that story with Henry. And although our skates were not silver, we had as much fun as Hans Brinker had in the book.

When skating got to be too much work on our ankles and too much stress on our backsides, we took off our skates and headed for the small hills to go sledding. Our sleds were the very popular kinds of the 1940's, usually pieces of cardboard or metal sheeting. But they worked just as well as the commercial sleds. Missing trees and stumps and hanging on to our improvised "sleds" provided challenges that heightened our sledding thrills and chills!

When the typical Michigan ice storms came and there was no school, it seemed we spent the whole day outside. And the winter cold didn't bother us at all. We were having fun doing things together. But Henry loved planes and he thought that someday he would like to be an airplane stunt man. I dreamed of being a pilot. So there were times when indoor activities seemed to dominate our thinking. Henry and I enjoyed building model aircrafts together. He imagined himself in a tailspin and pulling his Cougar up at the last minute and skimming across the heads of the spectators as they cheered and gave thumbs up to his stunts. In contrast, I imagined myself seated with my copilot in the cockpit as we flew a Trans World Airline to France. Where we got those dreams must have been from reading comic books or studying air travel in school. It certainly was not from movies or TV.

Henry's dad regularly bought him kits for motorized airplanes. We built those models in Henry's attic bedroom and, when the spring thaw came and the weather warmed up, we spent hours flying them around in circles outside. Small cables, attached to the planes' fuselages, ran to our hand controls by which we maneuvered the planes. I was good at looping and tail spinning the planes, but Henry was much better.

One day as we were assembling a P-51 Mustang, I asked Henry, "Why don't we design our own plane sometime?"

"Leon, I've got to concentrate."

The next morning we had that Mustang attacking an enemy plane every five minutes. We were ferocious.

The next time his dad bought a new kit for us, I asked again, "Henry, why don't we design our own airplane?"

"You don't give up, do you, Leon. Why should we come up with our own plans when someone else has done all the work?"

"To be original I guess. Just to see if we can do it."

"OK, OK. Design one and shut up," he said as he glued a rib in the fuselage. I chuckled because Henry said "Shut up" to anyone when he was concentrating.

I spent many grueling hours trying to design a perfect plane for us to build. A few days later when we were together, I proudly pulled out my design. "Henry, I decided we'd build a dirigible instead. Here are the plans."

He studied them. "Some blueprint you've got there," he laughed. "Looks like you had the pencil between your teeth and you sketched out a fence for a cow."

After a lot of persuasion on my part, he finally decided we'd try out my plans, so we walked to the hardware store and bought balsa wood, glue, tissue paper, and toothpicks. We cut the fuselage with razor blades, then mounted the ribs. We measured and glued and framed. As we constructed our Pippin-Cowell blimp, I asked him, "Will we be called creators or designers?"

"Neither."

"It isn't that bad, is it?"

Henry sorta ignored me and kept finishing the body. Then as we were gluing on white tissue paper, I said, "Henry. Stop for a minute. This is a serious question. God designed the universe. He drew up the blueprints as I did for this blimp. Only His were perfect! And he wants us to see him as Creator and know him like we know each other."

"You could be right, Leon, you could be right. But let's finish up, OK?" We kept painting and trimming it with red and white to be patriotic.

We never could get the basket right for the engine so we roped it onto the body and suspended the dirigible from the ceiling. I thought to myself that God didn't mess up his design plans like we did, but I didn't say anything more. The lopsided blimp was hanging, and his mother never said anything about the funny looking aircraft floating near the attic ceiling.

A short time later, Henry said, "Let's build this new model B plane my dad bought me. All the stuff we need is in the kit. Here, cut out the body of the plane. I need to study how to mount the motor. We've never worked on one of these before. And we're going to paint this one yellow."

As we were assembling the new model, I paused, looked over at him, and asked, "Henry, have you thought any more about God."

"Some," he said, and we kept cutting, gluing, and painting.

Two weeks later, as we were cleaning up all the mess from our projects, Henry, without a word, slid out of his chair, knelt down among all the glue, tissue paper, balsa wood, and airplane blueprints, and prayed out loud: "God, be in my life like you are in Leon's."

I was surprised because he didn't even tell me he was going to do that. With tissue paper sticking to my fingers, I knelt down and gave him a big hug.

"You satisfied now?" he asked me. He used "satisfied" a lot, too.

"Well, aren't you?"

"Yep."

Henry and I kept building and flying planes, even graduated to building the models that were remote controlled. No strings attached. And spent our spare time repairing the ones that crashed. Sometime we learned Bible verses while we steered our planes into nose dives and loops.

We went our separate ways after high school and lost touch with each other when I left for college. I wrote to him once but did not get a reply. And unforgettable memories of glue and balsa wood weren't enough to cement us together.

Neither of our dreams about aircrafts materialized. I became a college professor, and he a tool and die machinist. Years later I tried to locate him. Maybe in heaven we'll find each other and reminisce about kneeling in his attic bedroom beside the glue and balsa wood, I thought.

And then one fall day two years ago my wife found his name in the white pages. He was still living in the same town. I called him and our reminiscing began again. Yes, he did remember our assembling, gluing, and flying model airplanes. Yes, he remembered that we fished for bass and whitefish, and the thrill of pheasants flying around us. Yes, he did remember asking God to be in his life. And yes, he is still going to church.

#

Leon Pippin is a retired university professor with four degrees. He has written magazine articles, television scripts, and a curriculum guide for the state of Iowa Department of Education. He has directed and choreographed plays and musicals for high school, college, and community theatre. He writes a devotional blog, Guarded Hearts.net. He was awarded 2nd place for his memoir *Naked With Clothes On*, and 1st place for his poetry, *Haiku Cluster*, from Florida Christian Writers Conference 2015. Leon has four children. He and his wife live in Florida.

THE HOMECOMING

By *Olive Pollak*

Worst. Day. Ever.

On a Thursday evening, over thirty years ago, my father's phone call to my college dorm changed my priorities. The second he hung up, I knew my weekend plans were doomed. I'd promised myself if I completed all my homework and studied for midterms, I'd have fun at the annual homecoming event with my friends.

"What's up?" Rosalyn asks.

"My Dad wants me home tomorrow," I tell my roommate. "He says the police called. They claim to have my stolen purse. He wants me to drive the sixty miles to my hometown and meet him at the station."

"You never told me your purse was stolen. Thank goodness he called."

"No one stole anything." I reach under my desk and haul out my brown leather hobo bag.

"Are you saying your father made it up? It's so unlike him," Rosalyn said. "When I've visited with you on weekends he's always kept his word about everything."

"Oh, no. I believe the police contacted him. He'd never lie about something like that. I'm sure it's mistaken identity or a mix up."

"So? It's worth the weekend home to find out. I'd give anything to be in your shoes."

I roll my eyes and accentuate every word. "This is homecoming weekend."

"There'll be another one next year," Rosalyn says. "You need to rethink this. Your father loves and cares for you. He's someone you can count on no matter what." She lowers her head. "You are lucky. I have no family concerned about me. And no one to go home to on weekends."

"Miss the traditional homecoming? I'll be out of the loop on Monday when my friends discuss the happenings."

"Friends? You've hardly had time to get to know most of them," Rosalyn said. "I think you're putting a lot of faith in your new classmate bonds."

"Ah, you think I should consider them more like acquaintances?"

"I guarantee this, the first sight of trouble and they'll scatter like fall leaves on a windy day."

"You're right, my wise roommate. I should go home tomorrow." And I know Rosalyn will hold me to it. Too late to back out now.

***

At the Police Department, I unzip the plastic teddy bear shaped purse and peek inside. I see a tiny black stuffed doggie, a red colored pencil and a worn book.

"It's not mine," I tell the police officer.

"Look carefully at each item to be certain," he says.

I hurriedly fumble through the contents again. The furry animal, the pencil, even the purse itself isn't familiar. Tucked in a side compartment of the bag is a small leather covered book.

Could it be?

I lift the pocketsize book, study the red-edged pages and read the gold-letter title, New Testament Psalms and Proverbs. Inside, the first page is titled "Presented to" and penciled on the line beneath it, in my own youthful penmanship, "Olive Horning. 158 11th St, January second nineteen-sixty-two." Black ink scribbled across the bottom of the page, "253-4971", noted our home phone number for over twenty years.

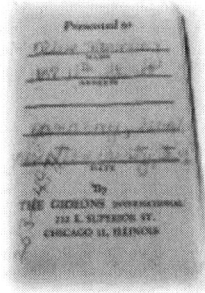

"Someone turned the purse in. We found your name and phone number listed in the local telephone book."

"But it's been twelve years," I whisper. "How could this possibly be?" I clutch the book to my chest as if it could disappear again. "Do you know who turned it in?"

"It was part of a stash of stolen goods recovered from an attic in one of your neighbors' homes. Mostly children's toys and valuables. We figured that over the years a youngster helped themselves whenever their friends weren't looking. Yours was the only one with a current name and number to contact."

When my dad and I step outside, I stuff the leather book in my pocket and offer the purse with its remaining contents to him. "Would you take this home and put it in my room?"

He doesn't take it from my hand, but says, "Why don't you bring it home and put it somewhere safe. You could stay for dinner. I'm making beef stew in the pressure cooker." He smiles wide.

"With homemade biscuits?" I ask.

He nods.

My favorite! On the long drive from campus, I hadn't stopped to eat lunch. I can't resist.

"All right."

***

I ease into a white wicker chair on our screened front porch and survey the yard. My father, the ultimate gardener, has bright red amaryllis, a healthy hedge of vibrant pink azaleas and abundant caladiums. A feast for the eyes. Squirrels and blue jays scurry among the massive old oaks.

I was born here. I spent many happy years as a child and into adulthood in this house. The neighboring homes have aged. But our 1950's brick ranch style home is solid. It's rose colored barrel tile roof hangs over the three bedroom and two bath home, one bathroom still tiled with the original Mamie Eisenhower pink and green bath tiles. The old jalousie windows have been replaced, but the original Florida Pine hardwood floors are still solid.

After dinner my dad asks, "Want to stay the night? We can watch David Brinkley's newscast and then the Andy Griffith Show."

"All right." There. I say it again. I don't even think about the parties after the big game. Well, maybe I do a little.

After a good night's sleep, I sit on the front porch with my dad sipping hot coffee. We enjoy nature and the silence together. So relaxing I almost forget to breath. Decades melt and more memories flow. My mother calling me for supper at twilight. The heartbreak of losing her to cancer when I was ten. Friends. Sultry summers. Even the shrill ring of our old-fashioned black standing telephone.

I'd sat on this porch when our mailman delivered my secret decoder ring. I could almost hear the chimes of the Union Congregational Church, one block away. My dad and I sat together on the porch steps to release lightning bugs I'd caught, our shoulders touching.

The memories overlap. I lean against the chair back and sigh.

Rosalyn's seen this on her overnight visits here. This is what she seeks and does not have.

The frenzied excitement of homecoming parties and dating have dulled for me. I feel myself relax as this rich discovery fills me.

On Sunday morning, I slide into my car. I see Dad pause from watering the hibiscus bush and wave at me. I wave back and smile. I ease off the emergency brake and memorize the scene. It's then that I realize that my very best friend is standing right in front of me.

As I drive back to college, the smile never leaves my face.

Best. Weekend. Ever.

#

Olive Pollak is a short story and novel writer and an avid reader. She has published short stories for anthologies with the Space Coast Writers' Guild, Florida Writers Association, and Brevard Scribblers. She's currently working on final edits of her mystery novel, *No More Secrets*. Olive is a native Floridian and belongs to Space Coast Writers Guild, Brevard Scribblers, Sisters-in-Crime chapter of Citrus Crime Writers, Florida Writers Association, and Mystery Writers of America

FRIENDS FOREVER

By Ed Rau

This is the story of two men who shared the same date and time of birth. They remained friends for more than sixty years. They were so close that most people assumed they were brothers. However, let me start from the beginning.

The year was 1924 and the location, Chicago, IL. Frank O'Neil was born on a bright sunny morning on June 14 at 7 a.m. at St. Bernard hospital to Richard and Jean O'Neil. Everyone called him Frankie from birth. Frankie was their first-born; they also had two additional boys and two girls.

The O'Neil family lived in the Saint Elizabeth neighborhood of Chicago. Their church was of the same name. Most of their fellow churchgoers were from Ireland as the city's Irish immigrants tended to reside in the same neighborhood. The Irish immigrants had a great advantage in America because they spoke English. Most of the other immigrants continued to use their native language as they had difficulty learning English. The neighborhood consisted of mostly working class folks. There were small clusters of Polish and Jewish people on the outskirts of the Irish ward as well as a growing number of African-Americans but for the most part the neighborhood was Irish.

Richard was a mason and worked steady as the city was growing and requirements for skilled labor were great. He was a hard worker, and insisted that Jean stay home, and care for the family. Jean loved being a mother and enjoyed doing the tasks that made each family member happy and enabling each to live life to the fullest. Richard always said that the Lord will provide for them and the care and protection of the children were their most important parental tasks.

The Saint Elizabeth community was their major source of friends. The O'Neil family attended church services and participated in church activities. The children attended Sunday school and learned their catechism lessons. Richard believed these tasks and participation in church sponsored functions were instrumental in the development and growth of each child's character.

The Metzger family is the other family in this story. Ethan and Esther Metzger were descendants of Jewish immigrants from Germany and lived in the Jewish sector of Chicago known as the Maxwell Street area. Isaac, their firstborn came into the world at 7 a.m. on June 14, 1924. He was born at Michael Reese hospital. His sister, Rachel was also born at Michael Reese four years later. Ethan owned a small food shop, which primarily catered to the Jewish population in the area but on occasion, some of the Irish families who lived nearby frequented the store. The family attended Congregation Ahavas Achim also located in the Maxwell Street area.

Ethan believed in the benefits of community gained from their attendance at synagogue services and activities. The preservation of their Jewish history and the lessons learned from active participation in synagogue functions and worship services influenced the positive development of the family's character and personalities. Each Saturday morning Isaac and his sister attended bible school and classes on Jewish history, customs, and ceremonies.

When the weather was pleasant, Jean would take Frankie for a buggy ride and walk to the nearby park so they could enjoy the sunshine and nice weather. While at the park, Jean would sit on one of the benches and sing to Frankie while rocking the carriage. She also watched the other folks as they passed-by. As Frankie grew older, he would run and play with the other children in the park. They so enjoyed their park visits that inclement weather was a major impediment to the success of their day.

One day, while strolling past Jean, Esther asked if she could join her on the bench.

"Excuse me, but do you mind if I sit on the bench with you?"

"Why no, not at all. Please sit down and enjoy this beautiful day." Jean responded.

This brief encounter was the beginning of a lifelong friendship for not only the two women but for Frankie and Isaac.

As the days and years went by the two boys grew close and spent many hours together playing in the park while their moms watched over them. In later years, their younger brothers and sisters joined them. The boys played on the playground equipment and, as years passed, included baseball, football and other sports into their daily routines.

The two boys were inseparable during their early years. Most people thought that they were brothers. One day while playing in the park a group of "bullies" attempted to disrupt Frankie and Isaac's game of catch by taking their football. One of the "bullies" grabbed Isaac who had the ball pushed him to the ground and tried to pry the ball loose from his hands. Frankie seeing this ran to them and landed a solid right hand to the "bully's" face. Frankie pulled the "bully" off Isaac and when Isaac got up with the football, the two boys ran off, as there were more "bullies" than the two of them could handle.

Frankie and Isaac ran to Isaac's house and told Esther what happened. Esther was upset about the incident and was thankful that no harm came to either boy. She then proceeded to lecture the boys about not fighting and the need to play well with everyone. She also thanked Frankie for coming to Isaac's rescue and offered both boys a piece of freshly baked cake.

The boys developed a special bond and often marveled at the fact that they both were born on the same date and at the same time. They discussed everything from their families, to sports, to their religion. Each questioning the other as to what they perceived as their differences.

Both boys went to the same high school and exceled in academics. Each achieving the honor roll multiple times. At graduation, Isaac as the class president gave the welcoming address and Frankie was the class valedictorian. Both boys played organized sports throughout their high school years. Frankie was a starting halfback in football and Isaac a forward in basketball. Each was a standout in their sport and the boy whose sport was not active at the time always attended the other's home games.

During one of Frankie's football games, Frankie received the ball and was to run between the right tackle and guard. As he began the run, the linebacker blocked the path and tackled Frankie. Both went down with a thud with each groaning loudly as they hit the ground. Frankie did not get up right away and when he did, he was holding his right arm. He fractured his wrist in several places, requiring hospitalization.

Isaac went to the hospital and waited with the O'Neil family. The orthopedic surgeon after completing Frankie's surgery met with the parents in the surgical waiting room. He informed them that everything went well and confirmed that Frankie fractured his wrist in two places. He advised the family that they could see Frankie as soon as he was awake. When the doctor departed, the group went to Frankie's room to wait for him to regain consciousness.

Football season was over for Frankie and he spent a number of weeks trying to learn how to write as his cast created a problem. His efforts while valiant proved fruitless. Isaac came up with a solution. He would help Frankie by doing all his writing including classroom tasks and homework. Isaac and Frankie met with the teachers to explain their plan and everyone agreed to Isaac's plan. This plan was to be for six weeks, which was when the doctor estimated he would be able to remove the cast. After the cast removal, the doctor prescribed physical therapy to strengthen Frankie's wrist in order to help him regain his writing capability.

The parents of both boys were amazed at how close they were and how each helped the other whenever necessary. Their friendship was special and one that made their parents proud. The boys' strong friendship also created a special bond between the parents and the other children. Everyone stood ready to help the other if necessary.

On December 7, 1941, the Japanese bombed Pearl Harbor. The United States declared war on Japan and sent troops to the Pacific. Shortly thereafter, Germany and Italy declared war on the United

States. The Selective Service began drafting men for the armed services. Isaac and Frankie were of age and both wanted to join. Isaac joined the Marine Corps and served in the Pacific. Frankie joined the Army and served with the Infantry in Europe. This was the start of a long separation for the two young men. Neither having the vaguest idea of how long the separation would be.

Isaac experienced heavy fighting with the Marines in the Pacific. He fought on Guadalcanal. It was difficult and deadly as the Japanese were solidly entrenched and heavily fortified. One fateful day, Isaac's unit encountered a Japanese firing position while on patrol. As the marines were advancing up a hill, machine gun fire erupted and hit Isaac. He fell to the ground thinking he was going to die. He thought of his mom, dad, sister, and Frankie. Boy, if he ever needed Frankie it was now. Isaac lost consciousness and awoke in a military field hospital.

A world away, Frankie's unit was awaiting orders to move on a German fueling location. He was sitting on the ground smoking a cigarette with the other men. All of a sudden, his body twitched and he was in pain. He did not know what happened but after a few minutes, the strange pain subsided. He began thinking of Isaac and felt something awful happened to him.

The Marines airlifted Isaac to the naval hospital in San Diego where he remained for many months recovering from his wounds. For his heroic efforts, the Marines awarded Isaac the Bronze Star with a V for Valor and a Purple Heart. His injuries were such that the Marine Corps discharged him from active duty. He remained in the hospital for an additional six months after which he became an outpatient for physical therapy.

During his time at the naval hospital, Isaac met a young Navy nurse. Lt. Martha Weingarten. Lt. Weingarten attended to him during those six months and provided whatever care she could to help with his recovery. While Isaac recovered from most of his wounds, he suffered permanent injury to his left leg requiring him to use a cane. Isaac and Martha fell in love during her six months of caring for him, and he proposed marriage. She was surprised at first but in the end said yes to Isaac's proposal.

Isaac's father passed away while he was in the Pacific. After Isaac was wounded and his subsequent medical evacuation to San Diego, Isaac's mother and his sister relocated to San Diego. When told of Isaac's long recovery process, Esther wanted to be near her son.

The O'Neil family relocated to Pittsburgh in 1942, where Richard found employment in the steel mills supporting the war effort. Jean and the children appeared much happier in Pittsburgh than in Chicago, Jean's biggest loss was that of her son whom she had not seen in almost three years. She wrote to him but most times, it took a month or more for the mail to arrive at Frankie's unit.

Frankie's mother and father were not aware of the death of Isaac's father and the relocation of Esther and Rachel to San Diego. The O'Neil connection to Isaac's family was through Frankie and during the war the two families never saw very much of each other. Thus, neither family knew the location of the other family.

Frankie mustered out of the Army in September 1945, with an honorable discharge. He received a Silver Star for heroism in helping save members of his platoon when trapped by enemy fire. After a short break, Frankie planned to use his GI Bill and go to college. He joined the family in Pittsburgh and inquired as to Isaac and his family. Jean told him that Isaac's father had died and Esther and her daughter moved away. His mother did not know where they now lived. Frankie wanted to learn more about Isaac but for the moment could not.

Frankie went to the University of Pennsylvania and received his bachelor's degree in business administration in 1950. While at the university, he met a nice young woman named Patricia Reagan and they began dating. After two years, they married in Pittsburgh where her family lived. Upon graduation, Frankie obtained employment in Philadelphia so the young couple relocated and established their new family.

Frankie worked for 30 plus years in Philadelphia retiring in 1985. Patricia became a homemaker after their second child. They had a boy named Robert, who was now 30 years old, and a daughter named Mary who was 25 and engaged to be married. Frankie was happy as to how his life played out except for the fact that he had lost track of Isaac. Now that he was retired, he made up his mind that he would try to find Isaac no matter where it led. The one big hole in this effort was that he had no contact with him since the war and did not know whether Isaac was alive or dead. Either way, Frankie was determined to find the answer.

Isaac and Martha remained in the San Diego area where Martha worked for twenty years as a nurse at the naval hospital. Isaac though officially listed as disabled tried several part time jobs just to keep busy. They had one child, a son named Ethan, which was the name of Isaac's father. During the son's early years, Isaac remained home with the boy and Martha continued working at the naval hospital. Ethan exceled at school and won a scholarship to Stanford, where he studied to be a doctor. On completion of his residency, Ethan established his medical practice in Carlsbad, California.

Since it was forty years since Frankie had contact with Isaac, he began his search for Isaac around the old neighborhood in Chicago. Most of the people he and Isaac knew either were dead or had moved away. However, Frankie did find one individual who knew Esther and Rachel. He told Frankie that the women moved away many years ago after the father died. They wanted to be closer to Isaac, who was in the hospital after returning from the war zone. The old man did not know where they relocated. Information new to Frankie was hearing of Ethan's death and that Isaac was seriously injured. Processing the new information in his mind, Frankie was determined more than ever to find his long lost friend.

Unable to glean additional information from the old neighborhood, Frankie went back to Philadelphia where he inquired about Isaac from Navy and Marine Corps offices in the Pentagon. He hoped that he would find additional information as to locating Isaac. The process was slow and required a significant amount of time but after several months, Frankie received information from a Marine Corps office that strengthened his motivation to find his long lost friend.

The Marine Corps' personnel office sent Frankie some basic information from Isaac's personnel file. Frankie was surprised to learn of Isaac's Bronze Star and his heroic deeds. When he saw the date, his mind flashed back to the episode he had back in Germany and one that until this day he could not explain. There was another very important fact included in the data packet and that was the order for Isaac's medical evacuation to the naval hospital in San Diego. Frankie proceeded to inquire of the naval hospital about any information they had on his friend. Caution was abundant as the military was hesitant about releasing any information on active and retired personnel to people outside the family. Frankie decided that he was going to San Diego to continue the search.

Frankie asked his wife to join him and they both flew to San Diego. Once settled into the hotel, Frankie began to develop a plan to get his search on track. First, he would go to the hospital administration office. Once he gathered all the information that he could, he would then go to the public library to search available city and public records in an attempt to try to obtain information that is more specific. He then planned to follow each lead in the hope that one would lead to Isaac or someone who knew Isaac's whereabouts.

Frankie and his wife spent five days in San Diego searching for Isaac and his family. They inquired at the last known address provided by the naval hospital. Since the address was active more than five years ago, Frankie was not able to track down any new leads. Frustrated by the lack of positive information, Frankie went to a nearby library and researched old City Directories and any other public reference documents that he could obtain. No definitive leads developed, and Frankie's scheduled time in San Diego was ending. Dejected, he suggested to his wife that they return home, regroup, and develop the next steps he planned to use in seeking Isaac's location.

After Martha retired from the naval hospital, she and Isaac relocated to Carlsbad, California, in northern San Diego County. Martha wanted to live near her son who practiced medicine in Carlsbad. Both Martha and Isaac were approaching the age when they felt they would begin to require assistance from others. Their life situation like so many others of the same age required them to be near other family members. This gave them the confidence that if they ever needed extra assistance, they would be close enough to have family provide such help. Isaac's mother passed away and his sister married and went to live in northern California. These moves provided additional impediments to Frankie in his search for Isaac.

Frankie never gave up in seeking the Isaac's location. He searched all documents and reference material he could find. The Internet was in its infancy, and most people were not skilled enough to conduct their research electronically. Frankie did find a reference in the Philadelphia library system to a Martha Metzger at the naval hospital in San Diego. He located a San Diego address as well as a phone number for an Isaac and Martha Metzger in an old telephone directory. He was so excited that he could not wait to get home and share the news with Pat.

"Pat I think that I have finally gotten a solid lead on Isaac. I have a telephone number and an address for an Isaac and Martha Metzger in San Diego," shouted Frankie as he ran into the house.

"Well hurry and dial the number," replied Pat.

Frankie dialed the number and eagerly awaited an answer. After a number of rings, there was an automated voice message stating that the number was no longer in service and Frankie hung up. He was disappointed and slumped down in a chair in the living room. He thought he had something this time, but no answer of the phone caused him to think he was wrong. Even though he had not succeeded, he was not about to give up. He stood up and said to Pat that he was going to go back to San Diego and follow up on this lead and any others he might uncover. Frankie then proceeded to book airline tickets as well as car and hotel reservations for him and Pat.

179

Pat did not say anything, as she too was eager to find Isaac.

"This trip I know we will find Isaac. I just feel it in my bones."

"I so hope you are right," she replied.

Once settled into their hotel, Frankie began following up on the information he gathered during his research back in Philadelphia. He began by calling the San Diego telephone number he found but again no answer. This time though, using the address he found in the old telephone book, he and Pat commandeered a taxi and went to the location. Proceeding to the front door, Frankie rang the doorbell. An old man sitting on his front porch yelled out, "There is no one living there. Place has been empty for some time."

Frankie turned to look at the old man and began to ask him questions about the last tenant and other facts that he had gathered about Isaac. The old man interrupted saying, "Why not come over here and sit for a minute and I will try to answer all of your questions without having to shout."

Frankie and Pat went over to the old man's porch and sat down. Frankie spent some time explaining to the man about his search. He went into detail about Isaac and of how they lost track of each other since the war. The old man listened, and when Frankie finished talking he responded.

"Well, I knew the man you call Isaac and his wife, Martha. While I was not a close friend, we were neighbors. They stopped to talk on many occasions. Mostly about, the weather or what was happening in the neighborhood. One day though, Isaac joined me on the porch and shared some personal information about his war injuries and his inability to overcome the disability and pain associated with it. He mentioned that he and Martha were thinking about moving to Carlsbad as they had a son, a doctor, who lived and practiced there. A few months later, they sold their house and were gone. I have not seen or heard from them since."

Frankie thanked the man for his time and the information he provided. Frankie could not wait until he and Pat were on the road to

Carlsbad. He felt he was so close to finding Isaac that he did not have a moment to lose. Within a few hours, they were on their way.

Arriving in Carlsbad, the first thing Frankie did was to look up a doctor named Metzger. He was in luck as he found only two doctors with a similar name. He immediately began calling the telephone numbers to inquire if they had a father named Isaac. On his second call, Frankie knew he found the right man. His name was Ethan the same as his grandfather and after a few moments Ethan agreed to meet in his office later that day.

Frankie and Pat went to Ethan's office with a positive feeling as to finding Isaac. After some brief general conversation, Ethan began asking Frankie some very specific questions about Isaac's early years. These questions helped Ethan determine if Frankie was really who he said he was. Someone who was very close with Isaac in those early years would only be able to respond to most of the questions and answers. After some thirty minutes of questioning Ethan was satisfied that it was Frankie, his father's closet friend since early childhood.

"I will call my father this evening and tell him about our meeting and arrange a reunion. I must tell you both that my father has not been doing well for a year or so. His disabilities from his wartime service cause him a number of mobility issues. His mind appears to be fine and he remains the same jokester that he always was. If it were not for my mother, dad would be unable to do very much these days. She spends the greater part of her day attending to him and when necessary driving him to appointments around town. Thankfully, Mother is in excellent health. Well, that is enough for today; I have to get back to my patients. I will call your hotel later this evening and give you my parents' address and the time you are expected for lunch."

Frankie and Pat thanked Ethan for his setting up a meeting with Isaac and Martha and departed his office. As promised, Ethan called that evening with the address and luncheon time.

The next day Frankie was up early and ready to go and see his childhood friend. He was so nervous and anxious to get started that Pat admonished him to remain calm and relax until it was time to leave the hotel. The couple departed for the noon luncheon in sufficient time to find their way to the address provided. The drive took approximately forty-five minutes. Frankie drove into the Metzger driveway at a few minutes before noon. When they arrived at the front door, Martha was waiting to welcome them. As they were introducing themselves, Isaac shouted from the living room, "Don't forget me I am in here waiting patiently."

The sound of Isaac's voice was music to Frankie's ears. Frankie hurried into the living room.

"Isaac, is it really you? After all these years, I am so happy to have found you."

The two embraced as tears welled up in both men's eyes. It had been so long since they had seen and talked to each other. After each man introduced his wife to the others, they all sat down and the reminiscing began. They each covered the years that they had been apart including telling stories about their wedding and of course their children. They talked, laughed, and cried for hours. The hour was late and Martha interrupted Isaac, reminding him that it was way past his bedtime, and suggested that they continue tomorrow. Isaac's health and physical condition was fragile and it was important that he follow the regime designed for his well-being. Frankie and Pat said goodnight and thanked Martha for her hospitality. Frankie also set a time for the next day when they could come to the house and continue with their reunion.

Frankie was happy and relieved about finding Isaac. He talked continually on the ride to the hotel reliving the day's events. Pat was happy for both men and stated how much she enjoyed her day. Driving into the hotel parking lot, Frankie became sleepy and very quiet as he walked to their room. Pat asked him what the problem was and Frankie expressed his concern about Isaac's health. She agreed but reminded him about Martha's profession as a nurse.

"Isaac is in very good hands with Martha, his doctor son and the

VA. I would not worry too much about him."

"I suppose you are right. Boy am I tired."

The next day was a continuation of the previous one. Both men laughed and cried reliving so many memories. Like most good things, they eventually end and so it was with the reunion. Frankie and Pat had to leave for home the next morning. As the visitation ended, there were the long good byes and best wishes. Both men embraced and with tears in their eyes promising to stay in touch.

On the flight home, Frankie remained quiet. His conversations were short and to the point. He was in no mood to be talkative and reminisce about what they had experienced that week. Frankie returned to his old self in a few days and had numerous telephone conversations with Isaac during the next several weeks.

One night while sleeping, Frankie awoke with a start and cried out Isaac's name. His cry awakened Pat and she asked what the matter was. He said he did not know but somehow he felt Isaac was in jeopardy. While he eventually calmed downed, he was unable to go to sleep. Early the next morning, Martha called to inform Frankie that Isaac had passed during the night. He had a massive heart attack and died on the way to the hospital. Frankie offered his and Pat's sincere condolences. Martha advised Frankie that Isaac's funeral services were to be the next afternoon in accordance with their Jewish faith. The timing of the Jewish service prevented his and Pat's attendance since they lived so far away. Thanking Martha for informing him, he said his goodbyes and hung up the phone.

Frankie spent the rest of the day thinking about his friend and reminiscing about their times together both good and bad. He was grateful that he had some time with Isaac just before he passed. He would never forget his friend and Isaac would remain in his heart and mind forever.

This is their story. Two men who were truly friends forever.

# # #

Ed Rau was born in Lawrence, MA. He is a 1963 graduate of Merrimack College in North Andover, MA with a Bachelor of Science degree in Marketing. He is a former Air Force Captain with Vietnam service. He is a Board member of the Space Coast Writers' Guild. Ed has contributed to several Guild projects/anthologies, including *Love and Rockets*, *Gratitude*, and *Spring*. He published his first novel, *Rocky Water*, in March 2016.

EMERGENCY EXIT

By H.V. Rhodes

When you spend a lot of time underground, you get very attuned to the signs of danger. For some guys, it's the faint sound of the earth shifting, or it's the water—a subtle change from the usual drip, drip, drip. Other guys can smell the gas cloud coming, before it builds up to a lethal dose. In any case, the first guy to sense something bad is about to happen will alert the others, and everyone will get quiet and still, noses up and ears open. It doesn't take a microsecond to figure out if it's real or it's nothing.

If we decide it's real, in another instant we'll all be running as fast as we can in a line, along the escape route.

That's why I was staring at the guy's butt in front of me, just as my buddy Fred was right behind me, all of us moving at the best speed we could manage. This time around it was bad.

Fred and I had been friends for a while. Down here, you have to find someone you trust, someone to keep an eye on your lunch or you go hungry. You do the same for him.

Things have been good lately. Until today, there hadn't been anything to worry about. I've had plenty to eat for a while. Maybe too much to eat, since I was having a hard time keeping up with the guy in front of me. In fact, even though I was sprinting, he was pulling away. I heard Fred panting behind me. I didn't take time to look, but I could tell he was really struggling. I didn't think there was anyone behind him, at least I couldn't hear anyone else, so we were probably the last ones out.

If we got out.

The aroma of gas got stronger. It was bad enough that there was hardly enough air down here for all the guys in the first place, but the concentration was starting to build up and there was much more coming our way.

Of course, this wasn't the first time this had ever happened, and we had planned for it. Every two hundred yards or so, there was a closure, so we could seal off sections of the tunnel. If you spend much time underground, you're always ready to get to a safe place in a hurry.

There was a closure up ahead and if we could make it there in time, we should be okay. The skinny guy in front got some distance on me, so much that I could hardly see him in the gloom. Behind me, I could hear parts of the tunnel fall in.

I got to the closure before I knew it. Maybe the gas had made me a little punchy. But we would be safe so long as we could seal the tunnel.

So, I was standing at the threshold of a safe place. I took a look back, and damned if Fred was nowhere in sight.

I waited for a few seconds, but the gas was starting to get to me. I was choking and my eyes were watering. But I was ready to roll the closure and block off that part of the tunnel.

Fred finally emerged from the gloom. He was moving slow. He should have pushed back from a meal or two. I knew I probably should have too, because the run had really tired me out. But I had made it to the closure while it seemed like Fred was just strolling along.

Doesn't he smell the gas? Doesn't he realize there's a safe place nearby?

That had been enough to get me moving at top speed.

Fred stared up at me with his wide-eyed look, as he struggled to get through the tunnel. I can still see his big eyes looking at me, as I grasped the stony surface and, with everything I had left, rolled the closure shut.

I guess I'll find a new friend in the next tunnel.

You may think you would have done something different, but you weren't there, were you? Did you really expect anything better from a rat?

#

H.V. Rhodes is a Virginian by ancestry. He served in the U.S. Navy and currently works as an engineer. He is a life-long student of the American adventure. His Civil War Naval adventure novel, *August 1864*, a SilverStowe Book, has recently been published by and is available at The Write Thought Inc (www.TheWriteThought.com) as well as Amazon.com.

A LITTLE HELP FROM MY FRIEND

By E. Lynne Wright

"Evelyn! Thank God, it's you!" Angela shrieked through the phone. "How did you know I needed you?"

"Huh?....You needed me?"

"I needed to talk to you and you called. How did you know?"

"I didn't," Evelyn said. "I was just calling."

"Oh, God, Ev, I needed to talk to you, but I forgot I can't tie up the phone. I have to keep the line open in case Tommy calls."

"Your brother?"

"Our mother's missing."

"What? Lina…missing?"

"Yeah she was supposed to come here after she left Tommy's place in Dallas. He took her to the airport, thought he had her all squared away, but when I met the plane, she wasn't on it. I phoned him and he bawled be out for not telling him she was senile. Ev, she wasn't senile when I last saw her!" Angela's voice broke. "Shit! Why is my husband always out of town when I need him? Is it some goddam law or something?"

"Where's Phil?"

"Denver on business," Angela said. "And our kids aren't here….Terry's in Columbus and Jennie's trekking in Nepal or some damned place and my crazy brother's in Dallas and my mother is God knows where! Oh Ev, I gotta get off the line. Tommy'll blow his cork it he calls and can't get through."

"Ange, he'll call you on Phil's line….Phil does still have that separate line for business calls at the house, doesn't he?"

"Sure, he'll call on Phil's line." Angela's voice was rising again. "Shows what a basket case I am. I forgot!"

"Okay," Evelyn said. "Now calm down. Tell me what's going on."

"I did tell you. We don't know where Momma is and I'm terrified."

"You said she was senile. Last time I saw her, she was sharp as a tack. What happened?"

"*I* didn't say she was senile," Angela said. "Tommy did. She's seventy-six years old, slowing down some, but she's not senile or wasn't."

"How long was she at Tommy's in Texas?"

"Three no, four months. Wait, there's a call on Phil's line. Can you wait?"

"Sure."

Evelyn's eyes wandered over the collage of photos on her study wall, stopping at a snapshot from their student nurse days. Two shiny-faced kids in the cluttered apartment Angela and her mother called home, in an old Pittsburgh blue-collar neighborhood across town from the hospital, their refuge back then, a place to lick their wounds and pig out on spaghetti.

She was what seventeen when she met Angela's mother? She remembered Lina, hunched over a numbers form at the chipped enamel-topped table in their tiny kitchen, the air silver-gray from unfiltered Chesterfields, an over-flowing ashtray and a coffee mug filled with what looked like black paint.

"Hiyah, Pops!" Lina's eyes crinkled, twinkling through the smoke curling around her face.

"Hiyah, Pops!" Evelyn sassed back. Friends, just like that.

Life had toughened Lina, but she never stopped believing tomorrow things would be better. Tomorrow, she'd win big at the numbers, get on with living her real life.

"Evelyn!" Angela's voice jerked her back to reality.

"Did you hear anything?" Evelyn asked.

"Tommy called the airport. Momma should have changed planes in Chicago, but she never boarded the second plane. Nobody knows where she is. If she were a piece of Samsonite, they'd find her. But they don't give a damn about a seventy-six-year-old woman flying coach, especially when she's not under a doctor's care."

"What now?"

Angela sobbed. "I don't know!"

Evelyn shivered. Her oldest, best friend, the 'tough cookie' everyone leaned on, was crumbling.

"I wish you lived closer." The voice was small, un-Angela-like.

"I'll be there in five hours," Evelyn said, doing some quick, mental calculations. "Six, tops."

"I can't ask you to drop everything."

"You didn't ask. I'm telling."

"What about David? Will he mind?"

"Ange, husbands love the chance to be slobs. Burping and not shaving and…."

"I don't know, kid. I can't picture that absent-minded professor of yours surviving long without you."

"Ange, I did the laundry yesterday, the weekly super-marketing this morning. He should be able to survive anything short of a nuclear holocaust for a few days."

"I hate to impose. If I weren't alone…. "

"You won't be alone for long. Hang in there now."

"Be careful driving."

Evelyn found David poring over some papers in his study and filled him in on what was going on.

"Could you get along without me for a couple of days, Hon?" she asked.

"I can get along, but I'll hate every minute without you." He grinned the lop-sided grin that melted her the first time he used it on her umpteen years and two kids ago.

"Angela really sounds strung out."

"Go," he said. "She'd be on your doorstep if you needed her."

"She would, and you're sweet to be so understanding."

"I'm a sweet and understanding guy."

"Modest, too."

"Yep."

"You will take care while I'm gone? Don't skip meals and stuff."

"Oh yeah. I will eat my veggies, wear my galoshes when it rains."

"I love you, David."

"Love you, too. Don't speed, Mario."

She tossed some things into a duffle bag, stuck a silly note on David's pillow, and headed for the Pennsylvania Turnpike, thankful for the pretty October weather. Brilliant blue skies; too early in the year for bad driving weather.

Driving from the flat, eastern part of the state, the road crossed the river at Harrisburg, twisted through the mountains, up to their breath-taking peaks, then down, sometimes through their blasted-out rocky centers. A gorgeous drive – if not for the reason for it, thinking of Angela all the time.

Poor Ange. Scared silly about her mother, then her spoiled brat of a brother heaps guilt on top of that. She remembered how after their parents' divorce, Tommy lived with their dad, squandered his college education, drinking, flunking out, while Angela took her genius IQ to a three-year nursing school. Even that was a struggle for Lina, who scratched out a living in their corner Mom & Pop grocery store, without Pop.

Evelyn wondered, as she often did since she was a girl in Pennsville and probably would for the rest of her life, why is was that most males seemed to possess a sense of entitlement to whatever it was they wanted, and females so often have a hard time believing they deserve any of the good stuff at all.

Now though, Angela and Phil coddled Lina in a small apartment attached to their home in the Pittsburgh suburbs.

She pulled off at a rest stop for gas, grabbed a pack of cheese crackers and a Coke from a vending machine. Gotta hurry, she thought. Angela needed her.

Mentally drifting back to their student days, it felt as if it all happened to someone else, long ago. Pennsylvania's lush, majestic mountains flashed by outside the car while demanding, arduous school days streaked past in her memory. Vividly, she remembered Angela mercilessly drilling her on smooth, striated and cardiac muscles for an anatomy quiz. Evelyn covering with the house mother for Angela who was on a date with Phil and late for check-in. Sneaking forbidden cigarettes while the whole gang argued late into the night about medical ethics, men, philosophy, and LIFE. After surviving three tough years, they were intimately familiar with life, disease, death and everything in between and when they finished, they were immature teenagers no longer and more than ready to join the exciting new women's movement.

Evelyn yawned, popped a Lifesaver into her mouth, wishing Phil were not away. He was her second brother. When she pulled into their drive, Angela was at the front door.

"Hey, kid, am I glad to see you!" She leaped down the front steps.

"Heard anything yet?" Evelyn asked as they hugged.

"Nothing. It's like she dropped off the face of the earth."

Angela tried to smile as they hugged again and took Evelyn's things from the car.

"Come on in. I'm so glad you're here! I'm going nuts, rattling around this house all alone."

At the kitchen table, Angela filled mugs with black coffee. They sat, grinned at each other, feeling all the history between them. Theirs was the kind of friendship that it didn't matter if they didn't see each other for a while. When they met again they took up right where they left off, their feelings for each other always the same. They didn't see the sags at their necks and the lines at their eyes that anyone else could see.

"I thought about flying to Chicago, but what good would that do? Maybe she's in New Orleans or Vancouver for all we know," Angela said.

"What's Tommy doing?"

"Making phone calls badgering people and stuff. He's his usual sweet, brotherly self, making me feel like a pile of horse manure."

"What's with him?"

Angela shrugged. "Contrary to popular belief, trouble does not ennoble all people. Geez, I hate waiting!"

"It's all you can do at the moment so calm down." Evelyn stroked her arm. "Fill me in. How're the kids? What's going on with them?"

"Let's see. You know about Terry. She's finally on the right track, we think. She's working and going to school and taking care of the baby alone. God knows how, but we're proud of her."

Evelyn reached across the table to pat Angela's hand.

"She's tough...like her mother," she said. "What about Jenny?"

"Our bad seed." Angela rolled her eyes. "After her brief stint with the Scientologists, she let her hair grow in and went trekking in Nepal."

Evelyn shook her head. "I don't understand trekking in Nepal. What's that mean?"

"You got me. Hell, I didn't even know where Nepal was before I looked it up. But there's more! She sent us a letter confessing she has an eating disorder, which scares me to death. She enclosed a photo and she looks like a skeleton with a backpack."

"Ange, I didn't know!"

"Of course you didn't," Angela said. "It's not the kind of stuff people put in their Xeroxed Christmas letters, is it?" She dabbed at her eyes with a soggy tissue. "It seems as if Jenny's taking a stroll through my Psyche textbook, saying, 'Let's see. I'll do this today and next week maybe I'll try that.' Anything to rattle the old folks."

Evelyn forced a smile.

"I'm not taking it as lightly as that sounded," Angela said.

"Hey, I know." Evelyn touched her friend's hand again, that hand with the crooked pinky finger, messed up in a volleyball game, a hand she knew almost as well as her own. I know you."

"Do you remember when the obstetrician first told you that you were pregnant? Remember how happy you were?" Angela said.

"Who could forget?"

"Did you understand then, that you were embarking on a lifelong commitment, and never again in your existence on this planet would you be entirely free from worry, due to the tadpole in your tummy?"

"No. And how charmingly you put it."

"But enough about my offspring. Now I'll worry about my mother!"

The wall telephone beside the table startled them, but Angela made a dive for it.

"Phil hi, Hon," she said. "No, no news yet."

Relieved to hear Evelyn was there, Phil promised to be home as soon as he could get away.

Strong, honorable Phil, the husband everyone said Angela would never find. She was too tall, too smart, too intimidating for most men. Phil was not most men.

Evelyn refilled their coffee mugs. "You still make the strongest coffee of anybody I know," she said.

"Remember how much coffee we used to drink when we were students?" Angela said.

"And smoked like stovepipes," Evelyn said. "Now, I can't stand the smell of cigarettes."

"Me, too." Angela put a bowl of fruit on the table. "You hungry? No? Geez, I haven't even asked how your kids are doing. I'm so self-centered."

"You've had a few things on your mind. Anyway, they're both okay. Davey's art gallery is doing well, confounding his parents."

"Nice to be wrong sometimes."

"And Carolyn is recovering from the insanity of a disastrous love affair. She's working part time at Davey's gallery, going to start classes towards her master's."

"Great." Angela's eyes were on the wall clock. "God! Why doesn't someone call?"

"Waiting women's lot in life," Evelyn said. "Worrying about kids and aging parents. What else is new?"

Abruptly, Angela jumped up from the table, grabbed the phone, listening. At the sound of the dial tone she slammed the phone back on the wall, rattling the dishes in the cupboard.

"Ange," Evelyn said. "Easy."

"Where could my Momma be, Ev?" Angela blinked back tears.

Evelyn shook her head, said nothing. There was nothing to say.

Angela dabbed furiously at her eyes. "Why the hell is it a given that human beings don't appreciate what they have until it's gone no matter what it is?"

"Now wait a minute...Lina is not gone. You don't know where she is at the moment, but she is not gone."

"Oh, you know what I mean. It's the same with the kids. When they're with you, they make you so damned mad sometimes; you almost wish they belonged to someone else. But if you're brutally honest with yourself, you know it's not entirely their fault and they are the way they are, at least partly because of you."

Evelyn sighed. "Yeah, and you can really drive yourself nutty if you count the ways they suffer because of your inadequacies."

She grabbed a tissue from the box, blew her nose.

"Carolyn?"

Evelyn nodded. "Actually, I didn't do a very good job with Davey either. When you get right down to it, I was a lousy mother."

"Oh, come on."

"No, I mean it." Evelyn smiled a wan smile. "If they ever give Shitty-Mother-of-the-Year award, I figure I'm a shoo-in."

"May I remind you those two turned out okay after a time?"

"True, in spite of my mothering, not because of it."

"So," Angela said with a smirk. "You're responsible for the bad stuff, but had nothing to do with the good stuff."

"Sounds dumb."

"Because it is dumb," Angela said. "I need a cigarette!"

"You quit."

"I'm gonna start again."

"No, you're not."

The telephone interrupted and Angela grabbed it on the first ring.

"Yes?" she shouted, then in a more normal tone, "What?...You're sure?...Oh, God!"

She started sniffling, but quietly. Looking at Evelyn, she

197

mouthed, "Tommy."

"Well?" Evelyn said when Angela hung up and flopped on a chair, deflated.

"They found her. She's okay."

"Oh great! Where?"

"Chicago. O'Hare. Missed her flight. Know where she was?" Angela's voice rose shrilly. "You want to know where my goddam mother was?"

Evelyn waited.

"In the ladies' room! She was in the ladies' room and didn't hear the flight being announced. Been wandering around ever since."

Fear gone now, Angela was furious. "She always did pick the worst damn times to pee! I mean, she knew when the flight was. Why didn't she go earlier? She's not stupid! And why didn't she call someone?"

"Ange." Evelyn gripped her shoulder. "It's over. Everything's okay."

Their eyes met and Angela sighed. "I haven't been so scared since we got Jenny's picture." Slowly, she shook her head. "I'm worrying about my mother the same way I worry about my kids. What does that tell you?"

"That Time marches on. That your mother's getting older. That *we're* getting older." Evelyn grinned. "Want to hear more?"

"No!" Angela rolled her eyes. "I gotta call Phil, let him know what's what. The airline is going to put Momma up in a hotel for the night. They're anxious to make her comfortable until they put her on a flight out in the morning."

"I bet they are."

"They will have her call me when they get her settled."

"Terrific. Everybody can sleep tonight."

"Geez! You must be exhausted – starved and exhausted. What time is it?"

They both looked at the clock.

"Gosh, midnight!" Evelyn said. "Eleven in Chicago."

"I'll call Phil and Terry. They'll be worried. Then we'll open a bottle of wine and have some food."

"Want me to start cooking something while you make your phone calls?

"You don't mind? There are those fake eggs in the fridge. That okay?"

"Great." Evelyn grinned. "I'll make them the way you taught me to make the real ones several lifetimes ago. Italian, with peppers and garlic and onions which you always have on hand."

She had a platter full ready with croissants from the freezer warming in the oven, wine open and breathing when Angela finished on the phone.

"You're an angel," Angela said. "I'm starved now that the pressure is off."

They clinked their glasses together.

"I believe the appropriate cliché is, 'That's what friends are for.'" Evelyn said.

Angela looked at her fondly. "You're one in a million."

"You've been there when I needed you."

"When? When did I ever do anything to compare with what you did for me today, dropping everything, driving hundreds of miles "

"When I was close to flunking microbiology and you drilled me on those nasty little organisms 'till they were like old pals," Evelyn said, her eyes misting. "You gave up your whole weekend."

Shrugging, Angela's voice softened. "I needed to cram, too."

"You helped me balance my checkbook when I got in trouble with the bank…and with my dad."

"You shared your dad with me and he showed me what a real dad is."

"Oh, Ange, you were always on my side, sometimes when it wasn't easy to be on my side!" Evelyn sipped her wine. "Hey, remember way back, when I broke up with Lionel? The guy who sent me one red rose every Monday, to brighten my week? I was so damned depressed when we stopped dating, I wanted to die."

"Never could figure out what you saw in him. Except for the rose, of course."

"You didn't tell me that, just kept fixing me up with blind dates."

"Which you didn't want at the time."

"But you insisted. Droves of them. Including that creep what was his name? The drip from LA? Clarence or Percy Mercer! That was it. Mercer."

Angela slunk down in her chair.

"In retrospect, I admit that one was a mistake," she said. "I should have known. A guy who leaves his shirt unbuttoned halfway to show his chest hair. In February. In Pittsburgh."

"Mercer!" Evelyn shrieked. "The boar to end all boars."

"He was bad." Angela nodded her head agreeably. "A slimy ego that shaved."

"How could you have sent me out with that pond scum?"

"It was when I subscribed to the Do-Something-Even-If-It's-Wrong philosophy," Angela said. "Hey, you said it yourself. That's what friends are for."

They saluted each other with their wine.

"'What though youth gave us love and roses, age still leaves us friends and wine,'" Angela recited solemnly.

"That's from Thomas Moore, isn't it?"

"Actually, I think I heard it on a Gallo wine commercial," Angela said, grinning.

"Whatever." Evelyn grinned back.

###

E. Lynne Wright is the author of eight books, including *More Than Petticoats: Remarkable Florida Women, Editions 1 & 2, It Happened in Florida, Editions 1 & 2, Myths & Mysteries of Florida, Disasters & Heroic Rescues of Florida, Mapping the Sunshine State Through History (with Vincent Virga) and Speaking Ill of the Dead: Jerks in Florida History.* Her nonfiction articles and short stories have appeared in the *Cleveland Plain Dealer, Hartford Courant,* anthologies and literary magazines..

TATTOO

By Linda Zern

The old woman clutched the paper bag of groceries to her chest. She was one of the invisible ones, a woman that men no longer noticed and young women pretended not to see.

The young man was hard not to notice. He wore his skin like a highway billboard advertising bravado and mutiny. A smirking pride filled his eyes when his tattoos made it hard for the soccer moms not to stare, and he laughed when their eyes slid away after he caught them looking.

Just as he stepped into the glare of sun in front of Nick's Fiercely Pierced Tattoo Emporium, the old woman dropped her *Save-A-Lot* bag. Groceries careened across the sidewalk. She stooped and grunted, shuffling after a can of cream of mushroom soup and two onions as they skipped like stones toward the gutter, but they rolled away too far, too fast for her to catch.

A dented can of creamed corn rocked near the tip of the young man's boot. Before he thought, he reached down and the can appeared in his hand like a weight, making his outstretched muscles bunch and swell. He could not resist admiring the newest ink on his arm. The tattoo artist had outdone himself. Dragon flame licked at his wrist, blue veins pulsed beneath arching neck—fire and fantasy and blood. Out of reflex and vanity, he tightened muscle and sinew and grinned as the dragon's tail twitched.

The old woman reached for the can of corn. Her skin was tissue paper stretched over pelican bones. Her frayed shirtsleeve ended at the knob of her elbow.

A flash of bleary ink caught his eye. A tired line of numbers marched forever between her wrist and elbow—blurred and blurring. They were a faint, fearful mathematics draining away into the thinning skin of her arm—dreadful.

He forgot to let go of the can and met her gaze above creamed corn and dragon's blood. The wrinkled line of her lips curved upward, but the smile did not reach her eyes, eyes like hollow pools full of nightmare answers to questions he dared not ask.

Her voice came on a puff of garlic and peppermint—an old woman's rasp, her accent a fragile hint. It was another clue as to what was done, and where, and when.

"Danke," she said, still tugging at the can. "Such a good boy."

"Yes, Ma'am."

"So proud your mother would be I think." She reached down, picked up the bag.

He placed creamed corn into the sack. She smiled while he pulled onions from the gutter and gathered the bits and pieces of her groceries back together, tucking them away. Finally, he pulled the paper bag out of her arms.

Shortening his stride, the young man with the new tattoo walked the old woman to a public bench. He waited in silence with her, escorted her to the bottom of the metal steps, helped her climb, and then watched as she waved goodbye from the window of the city bus—her tattoo a blur of ink and ash.

# # #

Linda Zern is an award-winning humor short story writer. Her chapter books include *Mooncalf* and *The Pocket Fairies of Middleburg*, an inspirational book titled *The Long-Promised Song* (which she wrote and illustrated), and a collection of humorous essays called *Zippityzern's: A Collage*. Zern's first full-length novel is *Beyond the Strandline*, a work of young adult fiction. She grows flowers, butterflies, grandchildren, rabbits, chickens, and horses in the beautiful countryside of Central Florida.

ABOUT THE EDITOR

Scott Tilley is president of the Space Coast Writers' Guild. He writes the weekly "Technology Today" column for the *Florida Today* newspaper (Gannett). He is the editor of the SCWG's previous anthologies *Love & Rockets*, *Gratitude*, and *Spring*. He's a professor at the Florida Institute of Technology and an ACM Distinguished Speaker. For more information about his writing, visit his author website at http://www.amazon.com/author/stilley.

ABOUT THE SCWG

www.SCWG.org

The Space Coast Writers' Guild (SCWG) is a network of writers dedicated to the same goal: helping you realize your writing ambitions. Whether you are crafting the Great American Novel for national distribution or penning an intimate story for an audience of one, you'll find support and encouragement in the Guild membership. Since 1982, the SCWG has provided activities to educate, develop, and promote writers and their writing. Dues are just $40 annually.

SCWG Membership Benefits

- Monthly meeting on the third Saturday with presentations on a variety of topics for writers

- Opportunities to sign and sell your books at SCWG functions

- Free advertising on the website and links from www.SCWG.org to your website

- Critique and special-focus groups

- Monthly bulletin to publicize your work

- Networking through the directory and activities

- Social media marketing and modern digital publishing guidance

- Opportunities to network with successful writers, agents, edits, publishers, and many more!

How to Join the SCWG

- Visit www.SCWG.org/join and follow the simple instructions

- Scan the QR code below to go to the website

- Attend a regular meeting or a special event

For more information, please contact the president, Scott Tilley, at stilley@scwg.org

Made in the USA
Columbia, SC
09 August 2017